May God ever bless you,
Luke Zimmer, ssc

The Apostolate of

Christian Renewal

Fr. Luke Zimmer, SS.CC.

I

The symbol of the Dove and Rainbow is taken from the Old Testament scene of the flood. Noah sent the Dove out and she brought back an olive branch, which is a sign of Peace. The Rainbow is a symbol of the promise of God not to destroy the world again by water. It is a sign of the Covenant He made with man. It is a symbol of renewal.

The picture of Jesus and Mary is used to show that the renewal of the spiritual life will come to the world through them. We are to go through Mary to Christ; with Christ to the Father in the Holy Spirit.

Printed in the United States of America
Tivoli Printing Co., Inc.
1803 S. Vermont Ave.
Los Angeles, CA 90006

II

Father Henri Systermans, SS.CC., Superior General of the Sacred Hearts Fathers presented Father Luke to His Holiness, Pope Paul VI in a private audience on December 17, 1969. His Holiness told Father Luke, "I bless your work. I bless you and anyone who spreads this apostolate."

Nihil Obstat:

      Rev. Msgr. Patrick Dignan, PH.D.

Imprimatur:

      Most Rev. Timothy Manning, D.D., J.C.D.
      Archbishop of Los Angeles

With Permission:

      Rev. Joseph Dowling, SS.CC.
      Provincial

March 23, 1972

Dedicated to Pope Paul VI and Pope John XXIII

"The Apostolate would lose its interior roots, its best forms, its highest ends...if the apostle were not a man of prayer"

Pope Paul VI

"Just as with the Teen-ager of the Gospel, Jesus calls you to walk with him; To offer your abilities, your efforts, your intelligence for the spread of his kingdom......

Jesus fed the multitudes with five loaves and two fishes and He knows how to use your contributions to the Apostolate, small as it may be, to work wonders."

Pope John XXIII

Table of Contents

I - The Apostolate of Christian Renewal

God is Dead - Hippie Movement

During the 1960's, we heard much about the theme that God is dead. We witnessed on a vast scale the so-called Hippie Movement. We all know that the hippies are those people who have dropped out of church, school and society. They were rebelling against the materialistic way of living that the modern world is pursuing. They felt that material wealth, power, and social acceptability did not bring peace, joy, happiness or brotherhood. We know that they came together and lived in communes so that they could build brotherhood by sharing with one another. However, since the modern world did not give them any spiritual principles to guide them, they soon fell into degrading practices of immoral living. They began to indulge in illicit sex, take drugs, alcohol and live a life of free love. They found that this did not bring happiness, peace, or joy into their lives. On the contrary, it brought many problems, and sometimes serious illness. They have had pleasure, but little happiness.

Jesus People

We have also seen another movement develop during the past few years - the Jesus People. Most of the Jesus People are former hippies, or revolutionists. However, now more and more other people are joining their ranks. These people have found Christ through the study of Scripture. They have found a loving person in Jesus Christ so they have become his followers. Yet they have found only half-Christ. When they find the whole Christ, they will find Christ's Church, too.

We can learn some lessons from the Jesus People if we are humble enough to do so. First, they prove to us that religion is important in the life of each one of us. Second, they prove that it is possible to live a life without sex, drugs, and alcohol when we put on Christ, when we obtain our strength from Him, or when we fall in love with Him and become His followers. The Jesus People also prove to the world that the life of celibacy lived by 95% of the priests, brothers and sisters down through the centuries is possible.

1

Religion and Psychiatry

An article of Bishop Topel in the Inland Register serves to impress upon our minds the importance of religion. Some years ago, Carl T. Jung, a world famous psychiatrist, wrote a book entitled: "Modern Man in Search of a Soul." In it we find the following statements:

"About a third of my cases are suffering from no clinically definable neurosis, but from the senselessness and emptyness of their lives.....

"How often have I heard a patient exclaim, 'If only I knew that my life had some meaning and purpose, then there would be no silly worry about my nerves...'

"A psycho-neurosis must be understood as the suffering of a human being who has not discovered what life means for him.....

"Among all my patients over 35 years of age, there has not been one whose problem in the last resort was not one of finding a religious outlook on life .... None of them has been really healed who did not regain his religious outlook."

Religion and Renewal

The Apostolate of Christian Renewal is meant to help us see the importance of religion in our lives; to help us to live our life with love, peace, joy and happiness.

We all know that Christ came into this world to save us from our sins and to give us life. We know that through baptism we share in God's nature, God's life and God's love. We know that through baptism we become children of the Father, brothers of Christ and Temples of the Holy Spirit. Perhaps, though, we do not realize that Our Heavenly Father should be able to say to each of us, "You are my beloved son, or daughter, in whom I am well pleased." In order to become a beloved son, or daughter we must become Christlike; we must "Put on Christ" as St. Paul tells us. This putting on Christ is extremely important for each one of us because only Christ can bring us to His Father.

2

The Christian Way

Christ came to us from His Father through the power of the Holy Spirit and the cooperation of the Blessed Virgin Mary. Thus, we should go back to the Father with Christ, through Mary, in the Holy Spirit.

Mary's Part in Renewal

We wish to foster a true, deep and special devotion to Mary in the Apostolate of Christian Renewal because she brings us to Christ in a simple and rapid way. She teaches us to know Christ and to love Him as a person. When we fall in love with Christ, our life takes on a whole new meaning. We have a purpose in life and life is worth living.

Christ said, "If you love me, the Father and I will come to you and take our abode in you." Then He will ask the Father to send the Holy Spirit. It is the Holy Spirit who is to form Christ in us. Our growth into Christlikeness should increase day by day, month by month, year by year and throughout our life, until we are ready to go home to dwell with God for all eternity.

The Christian Life

It is to a life of holiness that Vatican Council II is calling us. It is in order to guide us in this life of holiness that the Apostolate of Christion Renewal has been established. A holy life is a life of love, of prayer, of service to others. It is the Christian life. It is not meant to be pietistical. It is meant to be a complete, integrated Christian life, where love, rather than fear, where the positive, rather than the negative is stressed. We are to live with the freedom of the children of God, putting the beatitudes of Our Lord into practice. We do this by developing our interior spiritual life and by giving our services to others in the Church, with the Church, and through the Church.

Change and Responsibility

Vatican Council II intended to place more responsibility upon the individual for developing his spiritual life and for building community - the Kingdom of God. This is why

3

many things have been changed in the Church. The changes have caused pain, confusion, and even open rebellion. However, these changes should help us to become better Christians, if only we will be open and accept the responsibility of doing our part. Certain rules and regulations have been abrogated and we have been left to formulate our own mode of action. Therefore, some people find themselves floundering, trying to feel their way.

Program of Life

I wish to establish the Apostolate of Christian Renewal with the same spirit of freedom and responsibility granted to the People of God by Vatican Council II. Therefore I do not intend to have set rules and regulations in regard to prayer or service to others. Rather, I wish to give guide lines and suggestions which are *not binding in conscience*. I hope that each one who makes a commitment to Jesus Christ through Mary will have a deep conviction in what he or she is doing; that he or she will develop a program of life; a life of prayer and service. This may be worked out with one's pastor, spiritual director or confessor. Each one may act as an individual, but I would recommend that a group be formed in each parish, diocese, or civic community so that not only the individual will benefit, but that through united prayer and action, the whole community will be benefitted.

Renewal — Not Organization

I do not wish to establish another organization, nor do I wish the Apostolate of Christian Renewal to interfere or suppress any existing organizations. I hope, rather, that the Apostolate will supplement them. It is my desire that members of the Apostolate will join other existing organizations in a parish, the diocese, and the community. It is best for a person to join only one or, at the most two organizations within a parish, the diocese, and the community so that he is able to do his job correctly and efficiently. He should bring the spirit of joy, peace, serenity, and love, which is the spirit of the Apostolate into the organizations he joins.

II - Vatican Council II and Renewal of the Church

Renewal — Beginning, not End

Vatican Council II ended in 1965, but it served to be only the beginning of the renewal in the Church. The renewal desired by the Council is the development of the interior spiritual life of the individual person. It is the renewal of the Christian life by the People of God. Thus this renewal must keep on developing so that it will reach the life of the whole great ecclesial community. The renewal begun by the Council should be lived in the Church through the adoption of a new mentality, a new way of behavior, and a renewed effort at sanctification of the whole Church community and as individuals.

Individual and Vatican II

The question might be asked, what can the individual do in regard to the work of the Council? He should realize the importance of Vatican Council II for communities, for families, and for himself as an individual. He should realize that the Council documents, all 16, are the Magna Carta of the Church. He should avoid the dangers which would make the council ineffective in carrying out the mission of Christ. These dangers are twofold: One is that everything should be changed, and the other that nothing should be changed.

Everything Changed

A person who believes that everything should be changed develops an attitude that the Council began an era of such innovation that all traditional beliefs are no longer valid. He sees only the faults, defects, and inadequacies of those expressing Catholic life in the years gone by. He will work feverishly to set aside man, institutions, and customs and even doctrines — if they have the mark of the past on them. It is his wish to form a new Church completely different from the Church as we know it today. He will try to do away with all bonds of troublesome obedience and every form of sacred commitment. Such a person soon developes a spirit of intolerance towards anyone who adheres to traditional beliefs. The feelings of love and respect for the Church are darkened and he develops a facile sympathy for everything outside the Church. The adversaries of the Church become likeable and the model to follow, while his former friends become unlikeable and unbearable.

We should remember that the "Aggiornamento" the renewal of the Church by Vatican Council II is not intended to produce such disintegration of tested historical and institutional reality.

Nothing Changed

On the other hand the person who thinks that nothing should be changed confuses customs with tradition. He thinks that Vatican Council II was a mistake, a bad dream, and claims that it never should have taken place. He thinks and feels that the enemies of the Church are those who promote and adopt innovations even though they have been approved by the Church. He claims that tradition must prevail, no matter what happens. His mistake is really an excess of love, but this love is expressed towards brothers of the family of God as if they were unfaithful, or dangerous to the Church. An attitude like this produces division, hatred, and much uncharitableness.

Correct Approach

What is the correct attitude? What should a person do to bring about the renewal proposed by Vatican Council II? In order to know what is to be renewed, and how this should take place, it is imperative that each one of us studies the sixteen documents of Vatican II; that each one of us be acquainted with what the Holy Father is teaching in Faith and Morals in his encyclicals, in sermons at the General Audiences, and in his other writings or sermons. It would be well, too, to read and study the documents which come from the Bishops' conferences. It is well to remember that the official teachers of the Church are its Magisterium, the Pope and the Bishops. The pastoral voice of the Pope and the Bishops is not silent; the good hear it and will neither disregard it or neglect it. The entire community of the

6

clergy, religious and faithful should understand and support the pastoral function. There should not be two camps, or factions. Rather, there should be unity between the hierarchy and the remainder of the People of God.

Each of us should accept the co-responsibility of doing his part, according to his vocation in life, to build up the Kingdom of God. Much can be done through the parish councils by the lay people; through the priests and sisters' synods by the priests, brothers and sisters.

To achieve the full renewal of Vatican II, there must be a bond of Charity so that everyone will work together.

III - Knowledge of Oneself and Renewal

Vatican Council II has asked for a deep interior renewal of the spiritual life of the individual person. Yet, we should remember that man is not an island — he is a social being. Everything that affects the individual has an impact on society. Thus, there should be an inter-relationship between the individual and the community to bring about effective renewal.

Renewal means a returning, a going back to the Adam before the fall; in other words, a striving for perfection. It means that we should become aware of who we are, what we are, and why we are on earth. It is an attitude of one's heart, mind and soul. To have a renewal, a conversion has to take place; a metanoia, which means a change of heart. Christian renewal means that we become concerned with the things of God above all other things. It means what St. Paul said, "To put on Christ."

Dignity of a Person

Before we begin to renew ourselves we should become aware of our dignity as persons. In Scripture we read that we are created a little less than angels; that we are created in the image and likeness of God; that we are created as Kings and Masters of the whole world. We are also told by Christ, that we are greater than the whole world. Many of us might feel small and insignificant in comparison to the world, and all that is in it. But, if we keep Christ's words in mind, we will have a true perspective of reality.

Dignity as a Baptized Person

Our dignity as persons increased tremendously when we were baptized because through baptism we became supernatural persons. The waters of baptism washed the stain of original sin from our souls and we became the People of God; we became members of the family of God. We are the children of the Father, brothers and sisters of Christ, and temples of the Holy Spirit. The Triune God— the Father, Son and Holy Spirit dwell within us. Since we are members of the Family of God we are brothers and sisters to one another. We should be able to go to anyone in

8

the world and say, "You are my brother" or "You are my sister." Since we are children of the Father, He should be able to say to you and to me, "You are my beloved son, or daughter, in whom I am well pleased." In order to become a beloved son or daughter we must become Christlike, and this is the work of the Holy Spirit.

Share in God's Life

Something else happened at our baptism which is really beautiful - God gave us a share in His life; we participate in His life. This life is given to us in an embryonic stage and it must grow, increase and develop to maturity. It is hard for us to understand that we have spiritual life within us because we do not see it, feel it, or touch it. When we hold an acorn within our hand we know that there is natural life within. If the acorn is planted, a tree can come forth and develop gradually into a sturdy oak. We see the results or effects of supernatural life within our souls. How? We see the effects of love in our lives. This is beautifully explained by St. Paul; 1 Cor. 13/1-13.

> And I point out to you a yet more excellent way. If I should speak with the tongues of men and of angels, but do not have charity, I have become a sounding brass or a tinkling cymbal. And if I have prophecy and know all mysteries and all knowledge, and if I have all faith so as to remove mountains, yet do not have charity, I am nothing. And if I distribute all my goods to feed the poor, and if I deliver my body to be burned, yet do not have charity, it profits me nothing.
>
> Charity is patient, is kind; Charity does not envy, is not pretentious, is not puffed up, is not ambitious, is not self-seeking, is not provoked; thinks no evil, does not rejoice over wickedness, but rejoices with the truth; bears with all things, believes all things, hopes all things, endures all things.
>
> Charity never fails, whereas prophecies will disappear and tongues will cease, and knowledge will be destroyed. For we know in part and we prophesy in part; but when that which is perfect has come, that which is imperfect will be done away with. When I was a child, I spoke as a child, I felt as a child, thought as a child. Now that I have become a man, I have put away the things of a child. We see now through a mirror in an obscure manner, but then face to face. Now I know in part, but then I shall know even as I have been known. So there abide faith, hope, and charity, these three; but the greatest is charity. ....

9

Accepting or Questioning

Most of us were baptized when we were small. Therefore we took things for granted. We never became aware of our great dignity as Christian persons. We always accepted things on blind faith, without questioning anything. Or did we question whether God existed; whether Christ was really God as well as man; whether there is a heaven, hell or a devil; whether Christ instituted a Church? There is nothing wrong in asking questions because by doing so we are seeking answers. This should make us better catholics if we remember two things: to pray and to seek counsel.

A Doubting Christian

Modern man tends to accept doubts and act upon them without seeking seriously for the truth. He gives up prayer and religion without seeking help from others through counseling. How is a person who acts in this way going to find his way to God? It is almost impossible. It would take a miracle of grace for that. It seems that there is much intellectual pride in modern man. He wishes to find the answers for himself; he never wants to be told what to do or what to believe. If modern man is to find the answers he must become humble and seriously seek truth, and when he finds it, accept it humbly.

Don't Judge

Another reason for "Agnostic Catholics" is that Christians do not live as Christians. There is much criticism of how Christians live and practice their faith. This criticism is referred to by St. Matthew in his Gospel, Chapter 7, Verses 1-5:

> Do not judge, that you may not be judged, for with what judgement you judge, you shall be judged — But why do you see the speck in your brother's eye, and yet do not consider the beam in your own eye? You hypocrite, first cast out the beam in your own eye, and then you will see clearly to cast out the speck in your brother's eye.

Compare Ourselves With Christ

We should never compare ourselves with any other person. We should compare ourselves only with Christ!

Each one of us should look into his own life and he should ask himself the questions:

1) What does religion mean to me? Is it the most important thing in my life?
2) How am I living my religion?
3) Why do I go to Church?
4) Do I help others in need?
5) What prayers do I say and why? Do I treat God as a gigantic aspirin?
6) Do I realize that everything in life is a prayer?
7) Is my life Christ-centered?

Renewal Begins with Oneself

Modern man wants everyone to live as a Christian, yet he seems to forget that everything must begin with himself. He must be a Christian! Only the individual can decide to live as Christ.

We must give Christianity the chance to renew the world. This renewal is possible if everyone strives to live his christianity. Chesterton said, "The reason why Christianity has not succeeded is because it has never been tried." And Mahatma Gandhi said, "I greatly admire Christ. I could easily be His follower, but I have never met a true Christian." It is the duty, then, of each one of us to become a true Christian - An apostle like the early apostles. This means each one of us must strive to become a Saint like the Saints of old.

This is a Saint

Many people have a false idea of what sanctity is. They think that to be a saintly person it is necessary to have visions, revelations, the power to work miracles, foretell the future, read souls, and discern the spirits. They further feel that sanctity demands one to do extraordinary penances, such as fast, wear a hair shirt, or penance chain, or to scourge oneself. None of these things is sanctity. Rather, sanctity is doing the will of God in all things, at all times.

11

This means keeping the commandmants of God, living the beatitudes, stressing the positive and doing things from a motive of love and not of fear. It means to be a truly committed person.

A Committed Person

To become a committed person one must know oneself because a commitment is a mystery which can only come from within oneself. The responsibity of making a commitment cannot be passed on to another since it means a giving of self. It is a pledge of what a person is and what he will be. It involves a total gift which expresses the past, present and future.

Some might hesitate to make a commitment because they are fearful that they have to give up some things which they do not wish to give up. Others feel unworthy because of their faults, failings, and weaknesses. *If a person waits until he feels he is worthy he will never make a commitment.* A person should have nothing to fear in making a commitment to Christ through Mary because he has nothing to lose but his chains of passion and sin.

A Committed Person Contributes to the Well-being of the Whole World

A truty committed person can effect the well-being of the whole world. This was brought home to me very forcefully when I was in Holland in the summer of 1952. Every year there is a festival in the city of Nijmegen. The old and young go thirty kilometers from the city; the stronger people go forty five; and the very healthy and strong go sixty kilometers away. Then, they have three days in which to march into the city. Participants come from all over Holland. They dress according to the area of the country they represent. I was in the city of Nijmegen on the day in which everyone was to arrive - the last day of the festival. Naturally, not everyone made the full trip. Some dropped out along the way. The ones who did arrive came into the town singing songs, playing music and dancing. Each one received a small medal and the town from which the group came received a bouquet of flowers. As I watched them come into the town, I said to myself, "Isn't this just like

12

life - that is, the spiritual life? "All are called to live the spiritual life, but some drop out along the way." Then a desire to preach to everyone about the purpose of life surged up within me. In Holland, at that moment, the fulfillment of this desire was impossible because I did not know the language of the country. Even if I did know, I would have been considered eccentric. I wanted to help everyone in the whole world. The desire grew stronger as each minute passed. Then it seemed to me that God said, "You can help everyone in the whole world," and I asked, "How?" He answered, "You can help everyone in the whole world by becoming a saint." Therefore, I am convinced that a true Christian, a committed person, a saintly person can contribute to the well-being of the whole world.

A True Christian

Have you ever met a true Christian person in your life? I have met some. A true Christian person is one who is filled with deep interior joy, happiness, and love. These just seem to radiate from him because God's love has changed his heart and mind into a consuming fire which can enkindle others. When such a person comes into our lives, he leaves an impact upon us so that we will never be the same again.

Each one of us can be that committed person — a true Christian, a saintly person. You have to make the decision - What will it be?

IV - Knowledge of the World and Charity to Others

in Renewal

Prodigal Son and Modern Man

We are all familiar with the story of the Prodigal Son as described in St. Luke's Gospel, Chapter 15, Verses 11-32. It seems that the modern world is collectively living the same type of life as that of the Prodigal son.

The Prodigal Son asks his father for his inheritance and after receiving it he leaves home. He goes into a strange foreign land and becomes a loner. Modern man wishes to have material goods, and he sacrifices much to obtain them.

The Prodigal Son "Lived it up." He used his money to buy friends. He soon squandered all he had on loose living. He had pleasure from wine, women and song; but after his money was gone, everyone abandoned him and he found himself alone. Modern man lives it up, too. He uses people to obtain power, money, or pleasure. He puts his whole trust in technological advancements and squanders what he has received from God, from his fellowman, and from his own industry.

When the famine came, the Prodigal Son had to seek a job. He was hired to work on a pig farm where he had to feed the pigs. He longed to eat what the pigs ate. He felt the pinch of poverty and soon realized the need of his father. He repented and said that he would go home and say to his father, "I have sinned against heaven and you, I am not worthy to be called your son. Make me one of the servants." Thus, he went back in search of brotherhood, of freedom, of peace, and human dignity. Modern man is also feeling the pinch of poverty. He often finds himself alone because he has lost his freedom in licentious living. Modern man is also searching for true freedom, for brotherhood, for peace and happiness. He is looking for solutions to the confusion and frustrations in his life. He, too, is on the verge of making a decision and is on the way home. That is why the Jesus People movement began, and why the University students take courses in religion, and travel many miles to partake in sessions of meditations.

14

Father's Reaction

When the father saw his son coming home, he rushed out to meet him. The Prodigal Son said, "I have sinned against heaven and you. I am no longer worthy to be called your son." The father embraced and kissed him. He ordered that a robe be put around his shoulders, a ring be put on his finger, and shoes be brought for his feet. He commanded that a celebration of dancing and feasting take place. The Church must be like the father and go out to the people who are seeking to return. Each one of us is the Church so we must go out to our brother in need. We are our brother's keeper.

The Elder Brother

There was another brother in that story - the elder brother. He pouted, complained and would not have anything to do with the celebration. How are we going to react - like the father, or the elder brother? Our reaction is most important because we hear so much criticism, ridicule and uncharitable comments today about what is wrong with society, with the Church, with families and with individuals. What should be done? How should each one of us react? Christ gave us the answer many times.

Charity to our Neighbor

Christ said, "Love God with your whole mind, with your whole soul, with your whole heart, and with your whole strength and your neighbor as yourself."

To love our neighbor as ourselves demands much of us because it requires that we do not deny anyone what we would give to ourselves. If we practice this type of charity all negative attitudes toward every person would be eliminated. This type of charity is the beginning of justice. It means that we keep the commandments of God. By keeping the commandments we refrain from acting. Nevertheless we do a great service to our neighbor in living the commandments. This is the negative approach and thus is the lowest form of charity. Some of the commandments are positive and demand action, but most are the opposite. On another occasion, Christ said that we should love

15

our neighbor as we love Him. This type of charity requires much more than loving our neighbor as ourselves. This is the positive approach to living charity. It means putting the beatitudes into practice in our every day life.

When Christ washed the feet of the Apostles at the Last Supper He said, "This is my commandment, that you love one another as I love you." (Jn. 13/34-35) We are all familiar with the manner in which Christ loved us. He gave His life for us. For us this means to love our enemies. We are to pray for them and do good toward them. It means to forgive those who have wronged us in any way. An example would be the charity shown by Maria Goretti's mother in forgiving the man who killed her daughter. Maria Goretti gave her life in defense of her purity. Her assailant was imprisoned and later repented. When he was released from prison he went back to his home town and went to church. At communion time, Maria Goretti's mother and Alesandro walked up to the communion rail together and received Holy Communion. This was an act of true forgiveness. This is the charity demanded of us by Our Lord's commandment.

The summit of Christian love is to imitate the Blessed Trinity in our loving. It can never be a one way relationship; rather it should be a mutual love. Only Christianity has dared to demand such heights of love! That is, that we love with the Love of God! We do this when we will what God wills; when our will is in union with God's will. If we live this degree of charity we will have "Put on Christ" and we will be able to say "I live now not I, but Christ lives in me." This love leads to the conversion of the world because whenever anyone has a heart full of love, he always has something to give. This should and can mean you!

Beatitudes - Positive Blue-Print of Christian Living

You may say that is idealism, that is just beautiful words, but how can we put this into practice? How are we to live this? We must be positive and live our commitment in daily life. We do this by following the positive blue-print of Christian living; by living the Beatitudes preached by Christ in the sermon on the Mount.

"Blessed are the poor in spirit, for theirs is the Kingdom of God." I think that this means above all that we acknowledge the gifts, talents, and good points we have. It

16

means accepting the responsibility to use them for the good of others in need. We soon realize that we cannot do this without the help of God. Therefore, this makes us realize that we are dependent on God - thus poor in spirit. It can also mean that if we have material goods, we must not become attached to them. It is not wrong to be rich, but anyone who is rich has a tremendous responsibility to help those less fortunate. I do not believe that we should take from the rich and give to the poor because this causes resentment, hatred and uncharitableness. Rather, we should instruct the rich to freely give to the poor, always respecting the dignity of the person who receives aid. It would be a good practice for the rich to give 10% of their resourecs to the poor.

"Blessed are the meek for they shall possess the earth." God seems to choose the weak, the unlearned, the poor of the world to bring about His designs. Great things are done through the simple and humble because God works through and with them. He gives them the courage to do what has to be done, and the kindness to carry out the mission of God in an amiable way.

"Blessed are they who mourn for they shall be comforted." Everyone of us will have suffering in our life. It is necessary to carry our cross and follow Christ. Suffering, if taken correctly, can purify our souls. It can strengthen our wills, and it can bring us closer to God. We should look upon suffering as a blessing and not a curse.

"Blessed are they who hunger and thirst for justice, for they shall be satisfied." Justice means to give each one his due, but here it means much more. It means seeing the good in everyone. There is always "A little good in the worst of men and a little bad in the best of men." We should try hard to see the good, and to forgive the evil, or even the sinful. Yet we can and should point out faults, and failings in others. We should do this as an act of love.

"Blessed are the merciful, for they shall obtain mercy." Our mercy and forgiveness should extend to our enemies. We should love them. We should have compassion on others and show this in our words and deeds.

"Blessed are the pure of heart, for they shall see God." Above all this means that we should have a right intention in whatever we do or say. It also applies to purity, which is so needed today in our contemporary world. The people of the world need the witness of celibacy, of virginity, or modesty to remind them of eternal life.

"Blessed are the peacemakers, for they are called the children of God." We all should work for peace in the world. I feel that this should be done by trying to obtain peace in oneself first. If we are at peace within ourselves we can contribute to peace within a family. A peaceful family contributes to a peaceful community. The peaceful community contributes to peace in a nation, and the nation to the world. Peace must begin in the heart, mind and soul of the individual.

"Blessed are they who suffer persecution for justice' sake for theirs is the Kingdom of Heaven." Anyone who tries to live a committed Christian life will be ridiculed, misunderstood, persecuted and considered foolish. We should rejoice if this happens because then we know that we are followers of Christ. However, we should pray for those who speak against us - have mercy, and forgive!

"Blessed are you when men reproach you, and persecute you and speak falsely saying all manner of evil against you, for my sake, Rejoice and exault, because your reward is great in heaven." Anyone who follows Christ will be persecuted since he is not above the master. We should rejoice to be able to suffer for Christ, to do things for Him no matter what is costs. I don't think that we should do things just for a reward in heaven. We should love God and do what needs to be done for love of Him.

Helping others in Need

If we live the beatitudes we will carry out the corporal and spiritual works of mercy. In other words, we will help those in need. Everyone seems to be in need in one way or another. Today the world is a vast hospital and we see the broken-hearted everywhere.

Corporal Works of Mercy

1. Feed the hungry
2. Give drink to the thirsty
3. Clothe the naked
4. Visit the imprisoned
5. Shelter the homeless
6. Visit the sick
7. Bury the dead

Spiritual Works of Mercy

1. Admonish the sinner
2. Instruct the ignorant
3. Counsel the doubtful
4. Comfort the sorrowful
5. Bear wrongs patiently
6. Forgive all injuries
7. Pray for the living and the dead.

It is easier to do the corporal works of mercy, but the spiritual works of Mercy are more important, especially today when they are neglected.

Involvement

We all know that we are to use the gifts, talents and good things God has given to us in the service of others. The first duty is to share with the members of our family. Each one should contribute his share to build community in the home. This is done by praying together, playing together, working together and serving others in need as a family. We should try to become involved with the projects within our own parish. There are many things we can do. We can help with the CCD program, join the parish council, work in one of the organizations. It is wise to remember that we should not become involved in too many things, or we do nothing right. Rather, we should get involved in one or two projects and do the best we can in them. Some might be more gifted or have more time so that they can work on the diocesan level, or in the civic communities. We should all do what we are able to do for the good of the community. All of us can be mission minded.

10% to Charity

We encourage everyone to give 10% of his income to charity. It is just giving back to God what he has shared with us .It need not all be given to the Church. All works of charity can be included.

A Christocentric friendship

We should try to develop a Christocentric friendship with those we help. A Christocentric friendship implies that there be reciprocity in giving. Real sharing involves a two-way encounter. If the encounter is only one way, that is, constantly giving, it is no real encounter. It is the other person who must be made to realize, regardless of his condition, the need for himself to share.

A Well-balanced Spiritual Life

In renewal we should remember that we may not be so heavenly that we are no earthly good. That is, we only pray and do not share with others. Nor may we be so earthly we are no heavenly good. That is, that we share and become involved with community projects to the point that we forget God, prayer, or the individual. It is important that we have well balanced integrated Christian lives. We should do as Christ did; pray and share. We need to develop our own individual spiritual life, and contribute to building up the kingdom of God within the community.

As a child of God - *You* are the hope of the world! This fact is something to marvel at! Don't let the world down.

V - Knowledge of the Blessed Virgin Mary and Renewal

It is important that we have both a true and correct knowledge of Our Blessed Mother and a proper love and devotion to her. Vatican Council II tells us to avoid the falsity of exaggeration and the excess of narrow-mindedness in our devotion to her.

Exaggerated Devotion to Mary

Our devotion to Mary would be an exaggeration if we would make a God of Mary, or if our devotion would stop with her. It would also be an exaggeration if our devotion became something superficial, superstitious or magical.

Narrow-Mindedness in Devotion to Mary

On the other hand, it would be narrow-mindedness if we refused to have anything to do with Mary. The Saints never were so foolish! Anyone who would down-grade her true role in the spiritual life just to please others, or to make fun of any devotion to Mary as if it were magical, superstitious, or superficial would be narrow-minded. The same would be true if he looked down on people who have a devotion to Mary.

True Devotion Necessary

A true well-balanced outlook and devotion to Mary is what is needed in the Church. We should uphold the teachings of the Church about devotion to Mary, and about her place in spiritual living. The Church teaches that Mary is the Mother of Christ, the God-man; that she is the mother of men, and that she is the mother of the Church.

Devotion to Mary leads to Christ

We all know that any devotion to Mary must lead to Christ, and if it did not she would be the first to protest. Her heart was pierced that we could go through her to Christ. Christ came through her from the Father by the power of the Holy Spirit. We are to return to the Father with Christ through Mary in the Holy Spirit. Many say we really do not need Mary to go to Christ, and with Christ to the Father in the Holy Spirit. They are correct, but I believe that we go to Christ more quickly if we go through Mary. When we have a devotion to Mary we do love her, but she brings us to know and love Christ and to serve others in Christ. We begin to love Christ and to realize that He is a Person Who cares, who loves us in return. Then, too, Christ said, "If you love me, the Father and I will come to you and take up our abode in you." When this happens a deep love and devotion to God the Father develops in our spiritual life. Christ said, "Then I will ask the Father and He will send the Holy Spirit." We realize that the Holy Spirit is operating within us. We feel the presence of the Triune God. It is then that we can truly say God lives in us and we live in God. Many people think that this is the height of perfection, but in reality it is only the beginning of the spiritual life. That is, it is a growth in spiritual development.

Devotion to Mary is meant to be something Simple

To go through Mary is really something very simple. It is just an attitude of mind where we learn to offer all through her. It is a way of life which we should not make complicated in any way. But to develop this attitude of mind we need to know Mary. It would be well to study the Scriptures and the documents of Vatican II; especially in reference to Mary. We should also meditate on the mysteries of the rosary.

Rosary Devotion

Vatican Council II tells us that we should foster devotion to Mary, especially those which have been approved by the Church down through the centuries. The rosary is one of these devotions that should be fostered. Some people are turned off by the rosary because they think that it is just a repititious monotonous prayer. Yet, the rosary is a fruitful instrument. It was given to the people of God at a time when many were to poor to learn their religion in any other way. They could not afford to buy books or go to Catholic schools. I feel that we can learn much about Mary and God through the rosary devotion.

You may wonder why I have a special devotion to the rosary, or why I encourage you to say the rosary every day. When I was a young priest I was doing vocation work, which required much time for traveling. One day when I was driving through Rhode Island, June 14, 1955, it seemed to me that God said, "Father Luke, I want you to say the fifteen mysteries of the rosary every day until you die." I said, "How can I do that? I don't have the time. You know what I do - I pray all my prayers, travel many miles, preach often and counsel young people. How can I do that too?" It seemed to me that God said again, "Father Luke, you are to say the fifteen decades of the rosary every day until you die." My conscience began to bother me so I said, "O.K. I will say the fifteen decades of the rosary every day until I die, but you will have to give me a fifteen decade rosary." The next day, June 15, I met a woman who gave me a fifteen decade rosary. She said, "Father, I don't know why I have to give this to you, but I feel that I do." My first reaction was - "Oh, Oh, I am trapped."

When I say that God speaks to me I do not infer that I hear any voices. What I mean is that He illuminates my mind - the message is short, loud, and clear. If you study mystical theology you will see that this is the highest form of private revelation and it always comes from God. Only God can directly illuminate the intellect.

The Rosary and Peace

Many say, "You must say the rosary because God told you to, but we do not have to since He never told us." Is that really true? God can speak to us through angels, through His Blessed Mother, and in many other ways. And He did tell every Catholic to say the rosary (five decades) every day through the message of Our Blessed Mother at Fatima. Some say that we do not have to believe in private revelations. This is true. Yet, I think it is most foolish not to believe in Fatima. Why? Because the Church has said that these apparitions are from God. In fact, Our Blessed Mother told us that if we did not pray the daily rosary peace would not be in the world. Look around and you see for yourself what has happened. All the things she said would happen have happened except the destruction of whole nations. Let's hope this does not come about.

Rosary to be lived

I have learned from experience that the rosary can be a beautiful, meaningful, fulfilling and effective prayer. I have yet to find it boring or monotonus and I have said the fifteen decades every day, since June 15, 1955. When we pray the rosary we should meditate on the mysteries and learn the lessons contained therein. We can learn much about the virtues practiced by Christ, Mary, and St Joseph and we should then apply them to our own lives.

Mary's life with Christ

Mary was intimately associated with the mission of Christ throughout His life on earth. She fulfilled his needs while he was a child, she shared His hopes, desires and work in the hidden life, and was present at times during His public life, and suffered with Him at His crucifixion. In her sharing with Christ throughout His life she learned much about God and the things of God. She knew the hopes, desires and longings of her Son. She knew about the tender hearted nature of Christ. She has much to teach us if we are only open to her and let her take part in our lives. She brings us to Christ, and as at the wedding Feast of Cana, she will tell us to *do what he tells us*. This is the reason why I encourage everyone to consecrate himself, and his family to the Immaculate Heart of Mary. After having made the consecration to her, to live the Christian life, he should offer all through her to Jesus Christ.

VI - Knowledge of Jesus Christ and His Church in Renewal

It would be good for everyone in the Church, or in the world to take a realistic look at Jesus Christ and answer the question, "Who is Jesus Christ?"

Jesus Christ Superstar

Most of us have heard the record, "Jesus Christ Superstar." It portrays Christ as a doubting, questioning, and confused man. It seems that many can identify with Jesus because they resemble Him as He is represented in the recording. We all know the impact this record has made upon many, especially the youth. A movie is to be made of the material of "Jesus Christ Superstar." What impact will it have on society, on religion, and on youth? Is Christ really as He is shown to be in that record?

Jesus Christ in Holy Scripture as the God-man.

Let us turn to Holy Scripture and see what it has to say about Christ. At the Annunciation of the Archangel Gabriel we hear his words to Mary. "The Holy Spirit shall come upon you and the power of the Most High shall overshadow you, and therefore the Holy One to be born of you shall be called the Son of God."

At the visitation Elizabeth said, "Of all women you are the most blessed, and blessed is the fruit of your womb. Why should I be honored with a visit from the mother of my Lord?"

At the Nativity of Our Lord, the angels appeared to the Shepherds and said, "- - - I bring you news of great joy, a joy to be shared by the whole people. Today in the town of David a Savior has been born to you; He is the Christ the Lord - - - "

Simeon in the Temple said, "Now, Master, you can let your servant go in peace, just as you promised; because my eyes have seen the salvation which you have prepared for all the nations to see, a light to enlighten the pagans and the glory of your people Isreal."

When Christ was twelve years old He told His mother, "Why were you looking for me? Did you not know that I must be busy with My Father's affairs?"

Thus from the very beginning the Divinity of Christ shines through. He is more than just mere man. Yet, we know that He was a true man, too. Even His townsmen were surprised when He worked miracles and taught with authority. They were thinking of Him as a mere man and that is why they said, "Is this not the carpenter's son?"

Jesus Christ - a real man

We see that Christ acted as a man. He became tired out after a day's journey or work. He showed compassionate love toward others. He loves His mother as any child should; that is with a human love. He showed love when He wept over the death of His friend, Lazarus. He showed human love toward the apostles and toward all people. He loved humanly, yet He also loved Divinely, since He had a Divine Nature and was a Divine Person.

Christ said that the Father was greater than He, that is, in His human nature. He also said that He and the Father are one. This unity refers to His Divine Nature.

Since Christ was also God, He knew the sufferings He would have to undergo. He often talked about this. He carried his burdens of man within His Sacred Heart. We can readily imagine the inner sufferings He went through.

The moral character of Christ was without reproach throughout His life. He said, "Who can convict me of sin?" And the tender nature of His Heart was revealed throughout His life. He was kind, compassionate, and understanding of others' problems and of their sufferings. He was able to comprehend, to forgive, and rehabilitate. He was truly a man for others. No greater love than this does anyone have than to lay down His life for us.

Jesus Christ; God and Man

This is what we believe about Christ as Catholics: He is God and man. We believe that the Second Person of the Blessed Trinity took a human nature and thus Jesus Christ came into existance. We call this the mystery of the Incarnation. It is a mystery. We do not know everything, but we know something when we are dealing with a mystery. Christ became man so that He would be able to redeem us from our sins and to give us life. If He had been only God, the

26

Second Person of the Blessed Trinity, He could never have redeemed us; He could never have been our mediator; He could never have suffered for us or died for us on the cross. However, we attribute an action to the person, thus we can say that God suffered for us, died for us, and redeemed us because there is only one person in Christ - a Divine Person. To sum up our belief then - in Christ there are two natures: one divine, the other human, but there is only one person - a Divine Person.

Baptism of Christ & Peter's Testimony

When Christ was baptized in the River Jordan by St. John the Baptist, the heavens opened and the voice of the Father was heard saying, "This is my Beloved Son in whom I am well pleased." In His public life Christ asked the Apostles, "Who do people say the Son of man is?" He speaks in the third person rather than the first. He calls Himself the son of man. When Matthew uses that term he lets the Divinity of Christ shine through. The Apostles answered, "Some say John the Baptist, Eliah, Jeremiah, or one of the prophets." Then Christ said, "Who do you say I am?" It was Simon Peter who answered, "You are the Messiah, the Son of the Living God." Christ made it clear that Peter's answer was equivalent to a confession of His Divine Sonship. "Blessed are you, Simon-bar-Jona, for flesh and blood have not revealed this to you but *my Father who is in Heaven*."

Mission of Christ

Christ's mission was to preach the Gospel to all men; that is, to tell the truth and spread the Good news. This mission was to be carried on after His death so He chose the Apostles and gave them the same mission He received from His Father. He appointed Peter to be head of His Church. He made it clear that Peter was chosen because the Father had revealed to Peter who Christ was. "And I say to you, you are Peter, and upon this rock I will build my Church, and the gates of hell shall not prevail against it. And I give to you the keys of the Kingdom of Heaven; and whatsoever you shall loose on earth shall be loosed in heaven."

Primacy of Peter

We all know that Peter was not a rock. He was far from it. Rather he was weak, a simple fisherman. He was kind and well-intentioned, but rash, impulsive and at times even cowardly. The Rock referred to was the Primacy of Peter. Peter was intended to be the Pope, the Vicar of Christ and Head of the Church. Christ established an heirarical Church and not a democratic Church.

The Pope - Faith and Morals

Many speak against the Pope and ask how he can teach faith and morals without error? After all, he is a man as we are. He has his faults, failings, and weaknesses. He suffers temptations just as we do. All this is true. In the past some Popes have made mistakes in their private lives, in their teachings on matters other than faith and morals. When the Holy Father speaks about history, or science or any other subject he can make mistakes and has done so. If we say that the Pope has no right to speak on faith and morals we call Christ a liar - He gave the Pope the command to teach all things He taught the Apostles, and He promised the Holy Spirit would guide him. Therefore anyone who speaks against the Pope when he is speaking on faith and morals is not speaking against the Pope. He is speaking against the Holy Spirit.

Greatest Love Story

When we read the life of Christ as revealed in Scripture we are reading the greatest love story ever told. It was the love of the Sacred Heart of Jesus that strengthened Him to undergo sufferings throughout His life. His inner feelings and sufferings were openly expressed in the scene of the Garden of Gethsemane. Yet, he did not question the purpose of His sufferings. No! He only asked the Father to remove the sufferings if it were possible. He always said after His request, "Not my will, but thine be done." The love of the Sacred Heart of Jesus impelled Him to undergo the trial, the ordeal of carrying the cross, and the crucifixion. The love of the Sacred Heart made Him utter the words of mercy and forgiveness while on the cross. The love of the Sacred Heart was manifested after the resurrection when He promised to send the Holy Spirit to guide the Church.

The Church - A Gift from Christ

The Church is a gift to man from the Sacred Heart of Jesus. It is through the Church, her teachings and sacraments that we are to arrive at that holiness of life desired by Vatican II. Thus we gladly accept the Church and all that this entails.

The Sacred Heart of Jesus gave us the Liturgy and Holy Communion. He is present in His risen state in the Blessed Sacrament of the Altar. His Heart is filled with compassion, love and mercy for each one of us. He wishes to extend His love into our lives and into our families.

Commitment to Christ

All of us can let Christ's love come into our lives if we make a total commitment to Him. That is, we must give to Him completely and live our lives for Him. When we give ourselves to Jesus it means to give ourselves to others to love them in Him. We give ourselves to Him in our neighbor.

"Amen, amen, I say to you as long as you did anything to the least of those who believe in me, you did it for me." (Mt. 25/40)

Covenant with the Family

We can let His love flow into our families by having the Enthronement of the Sacred Heart in our home. By doing this we are making a covenant with Christ. We are saying, you are our God, and we are your people, your family. We are promising the Sacred Heart to be faithful to this covenant - to live a truly Christian life.

VII - Liturgy and Holy Communion in Renewal

During the past few years, encounter groups, group dynamics and sensitivity sessions are the very much "in thing"; they are the rage of society. However, long before the reign of modern psychology, group dynamics and sensitivity training people encountered Jesus Christ. When they encountered Jesus Christ they had to be truly themselves and they had to become His followers.

> "Then bringing their boats back to land, the left everything and followed Him" (Lk 5/11)

Liturgy - Encountering Jesus Christ

The liturgy is an encounter with Jesus Christ. It is an encounter God designs for each one of us. Through this encounter we are to become Christlike. Yet, is the liturgy an encounter in reality for all of us, or just a few of us?

There are many reasons why the People of God go to the liturgy. Some go in obedience to religious tradition; the Church says they must go, therefore they go. Others go only because their fathers went, and they wish to keep the faith and practices of their parents. Perhaps many go through fear of what may happen to them if they do not go. They fear something may happen to them in this world or after death. It may be that some go only for excitement and entertainment, or to be with their friends. Some may even go to give the impression that they are better than they are. Others go for their spiritual refreshment for the week, or because they feel that by going they contribute to building up the moral fiber of society. Through participation in the liturgy they feel they do their bit to hold off the moral chaos of the world.

These are some reasons why people go to church. They are not all bad, but they are not distinctly Christian reasons. They are not necessarily connected with Christ. We should come to the liturgy to encounter Christ.

Christianity in Particular

We begin to understand the Liturgy when we come not for "Religion in general," but for a commitment to Jesus Christ in particular. We were baptized to be followers of Jesus Christ.

30

"Brothers, I want to remind you of the Gospel I preached to you, the gospel that you received and in which you are firmly established; because the gospel will save you only if you keep believing exactly what I preached to you. Believing anything else will not lead to anything." (1 Cor. 15/12)

Religion in general may be inspiring and uplifting, but true liberation is found in communion with the Victorious Christ, and that is accomplished in the Liturgy.

America has become a mass society. Distinctiveness and particularity are discouraged so that there is a trend toward generalized mediocrity. The chief imperative is to go along with the crowd - do not make a decision or a commitment. By T.V. commercials, we are asked to make many trivial decisions, for example, what deoderant we will use, what cat food we will buy, what soap we will use. None of these is a true decision, a real commitment.

American religion has also succumed to mass culture. A leading political figure said a few years ago - "Worship the God of your choice. It does not matter what you believe as long as you believe." This is religion in general and must necessarily resist any real encounter with Jesus Christ. He is too particular, too insistent, too purposeful.

The Liturgy challenges the mind to abandon the horde, to get specific about the issues of life and death. We do not believe in religion in general. Christianity is embarrassingly particular. In the Creed we say —"We believe in God the Father Almighty — and Jesus Christ His only Son—"

We see what happened with Peter, James, and John at the Transfiguration when they encountered Christ in His Divine Personality. They were never the same again. It is dangerous to encounter Christ because then we have to change. No wonder there is so much resistance. Biblical language asks for a conversion, a rebirth as a new person. For the smug and satisfied this prospect can only be threatening but for those who hunger and thirst for righteousness an encounter with Christ means only a liberation, a losing of their chains.

The Liturgy is an encounter with Christ. We are with Him at Calvary. At the Last Supper Christ instituted the Sacrament of His Body and Blood to perpetuate the Sacrifice of the Cross throughout the centuries until He comes again. In this way honor and glory is offered to the Father by the priests from the rising of the sun unto the setting thereof.

Priesthood of Christ, the Ministerial Priesthood and the Common Priesthood

The People of God exercise their priesthood whenever they participate in offering the Eucharistic Sacrificial banquet. They are able to unite themselves, their lives, their work and all creation with the Divine Victim, and thus consecrate the world to God.

We all know that there is only one priest - Jesus Christ, At the Last Supper Christ gave the Apostles the power to share in His Priesthood. Thus the ministerial priesthood came into being. Christ could never again exercise His Priesthood without the ministerial priest, but only because He willed it to be that way. The faithful participate in the priesthood of Christ, too. They were given a share in Christ's priesthood when they were baptized. They, too, cannot exercise their priesthood without the ministerial priest. That is why they go to church for the liturgy. The liturgy is the highest form of community sacrifical celebration. Therefore no one should feel obligated to go to the liturgy. Rather, he should feel honored. No one acts alone, but as a member of the family of God, as a community. The Eucharistic sacrificial banquet is a united prayer of Christ and the faithful. We are also united with the communion of Saints at the liturgy.

Liturgical Changes and Meaning

The Vatican Council has reformed the mass, that is the liturgy. The altar has been changed so that it faces the faithful, and the liturgy is in the vernacular so that the people can more fully participate in the liturgy. Through this participation they fulfill their priesthood.

The liturgy is divided into two parts: the liturgy of the word, and the Liturgy of the Eucharist. Each part is equally important and both parts form one liturgical action. In the liturgy of the word we profess our sinfullness, and ask forgiveness; we sing the praises of the Lord in the Gloria; in the readings and the gospel, God speaks to us; and in the homily the word of god is explained to the people of God. Then we all proclaim our belief in the doctrines of the faith by reciting the creed. We end the liturgy of the word with the petitions of the prayer of the faithful.

The liturgy of the Eucharist begins with the offertory procession; the offering of the gifts of bread and wine. At the offertory we should offer ourselves to God. The Canon is the apex of the Eucharistic service. At the moment of the consecration the sacrifice takes place and Christ becomes present Body, Blood, Soul and Divinity in the Blessed Sacrament of the altar. The banquet of Our Lord begins with the Our Father, and Christ becomes our spiritual food in Holy Communion. The period of thanksgiving is important, too, in the liturgy. It is a time of silent prayer where we can express our gratitude for such a great gift, favor and privilege. When we leave the liturgical service we should take Christ back into the world with us.

The Mass is ever old and new. It is a victory over death and sin. It is really Good Friday, Easter Sunday and the Ascension rolled into one. It is the sign of our covenant with Our Lord. It really should be the center of our day and of our life.

Adoration of Christ in the Blessed Sacrament

Christ has a deep abiding love for us and that is why He wished to remain with us in the Blessed Sacrament of the Altar. Therefore, there is a place for adoration of the Blessed Sacrament of the Altar. His remaining with us in the Blessed Sacrament is a sign of His fidelity to the covenant He made with man. It would be a wonderful practice to spend five minutes retreat before the Blessed Sacrament every day. It is there, too, that we can and should make reparation for the sins of mankind.

Daily Mass

Those who are able should also make a practice of going to daily Mass. Attendance at daily Mass is no longer difficult. The work day is much shorter, churches are more plentiful, and transportation, even if one does not drive a car, is faster and more convenient. In the larger cities there are usually weekday noon hour or late afternoon masses in downtown and suburban churches for those who cannot attend early morning services.

VIII - Sacrament of Reconcilation and Renewal

A Change of Heart

St. John the Baptist called for a repentence, a conversion from a former way of living. A conversion can mean a change from one religion to another; or from paganism to Christianity; or it can mean the abandoning of a former sinful life for a life of holiness. It is really a metanoia which is a change of heart affecting the entire personality, reaching the very roots of the soul, changing one's whole orientation and approach to life. It means living one's whole life in an entirely different way. This was St. John the Baptist's message in asking people to be baptized. He was asking them to make a total commitment to God.

Love of Christ for man demands a return of Love.

Christ came into the world and offered Himself so that sin could be forgiven and supernatural life be given and increased. Actually He demanded the same thing St. John the Baptist did, that is a complete change of heart. He asks people to make a total commitment of themselves to Him.

Compassion of Jesus Christ for man.

Christ always showed compassion upon people who were suffering. However, His healing miraculous powers were not just an expression of compassion for human suffering. He did not take all the suffering and difficulty out of human life. He also suffered in order to reach us, to bring us back to God, and to forgive us our sins. Christ knew human nature with its weaknesses, ignorance, prejudices, faults and failings. Therefore He had compassion on us and gave us the Sacrament of Reconciliation to help us overcome these things. He wanted to give us peace, joy and happiness.

When Jesus Christ worked miracles He showed forth the power of God within Himself. He also showed He was God by forgiving sins. This power of forgiving sins belongs only to God. He forgave the sins of the paralytic before curing him. The Pharises wondered how He could forgive sins, for they thought only God can forgive sins. Christ answered their incredulity eloquently as we read in scripture. Jesus Christ gave this power to forgive sins to the apostles when He said, "Receive the Holy Spirit; whose sins you shall forgive, they are forgiven them; whose sins you shall retain, they are retained." (Jn 20/23)

Why go to Confession?

Many question today, how a man can forgive sins? I can tell my sins to God, why should I tell them to a priest? The only answer we can give is that it is the will of Jesus Christ that priests forgive sins, and that people should use the sacrament of penance.

Mercy of God

A few years ago it was hard to preach on the mercy of God in forgiving sins. We had to plead with people for them to believe that they were forgiven, and to forget the past. People felt the weight of their sins and had a hard time forgiving themselves. Therefore it was hard for them to believe that God forgave them.

Today it is also hard to preach about the mercy of God in forgiving sin because modern man does not feel a need for mercy. He has lost the sense of God. Therefore, he has lost the sense of sin. During the past few years, there has not been an area of traditional morality that has not been challenged, watered down, explained away by someone or other. It is an amazing fact that when any norm or principle of morality is challenged, questioned, or denied by a teacher, theologian, preacher or writer his word becomes law, and the teaching of the Church is disregarded. It is easy to accept that which is pleasing to our fallen nature. Yet, if we do this, we simply follow the pied pipers of our day.

St. John's Epistle begins in a warm and personal way -

"What we are writing is what we have seen, what it was that met our gaze and the touch of our hands. Yes, life dawned; and it is as eyewitnesses that we bring you news of that life, that eternal life, which abode at first with the Father, and has dawned now on us" —

Then he says, "Brethern, sin is with us. If we deny that, we are making God a liar. It means that the truth does not dwell in us. No, it is when we confess our sins that he forgives us our sins, ever true to His promise, ever dealing right with us, and all our wrong-doing is purged away"

We cannot just take part of Jesus Christ's doctrine. We have to accept all He teaches. We do have a need for a redeemer. Otherwise, Jesus Christ's life, His passion, and His resurrection have no meaning. It seems that we have two types of people in the world today. Those who know that they are sinners, and those who believe that they are without sin, and are not capable of sinning. The Saints were never so foolish. They were keenly aware of their sinfulness, and ever conscious of their weakness.

St. Paul shows us that he was aware of his weakness and sinfullness. "Who will deliver us from the bondage of this nature? The good things I want to do, I do not do; and the evil that I would not, that I do." Then he goes on and answers the question for us — it is God's grace that delivers us from sin, and that grace comes to us in the Sacrament of reconciliation.

Apathy in Spiritual Living

We all know that confessions have dropped off in the past few years. Is this good? Are we better than our parents, or their parents? Or are we losing our faith, and thus losing the sense of sin? Are we really better for not going to confession frequently? There is spiritual apathy in the air. Perhaps because we are living in an affluent society, we tend to forget about God. I gave a retreat to the lepers of Molokai in Hawaii. I found out that only one third went to church. They said they knew they were doing wrong, but they believed that they could live a long life. The new medicine arrests the advancement of the sickness so they could live quite a full life. They said that they would come to God in their own good time. Many of us today might feel the same way. However, when we stay away from God, soon the thoughts of Him grow dim. The more we forget about God the less we

37

think about Satan. It seems that people are afraid to mention his existence - to them it sounds so medieval. Our Lord spoke often of the devil and we know that he is real - as real as sin.

Read the headlines any day of the week and you will see that there is sin in the world on a vast scale. The power of the evil one is manifested clearly for all to see if we do not blind ourselves deliberately.

St. Paul tells us, "It is not against flesh and blood that we enter the lists, but against principalities, and powers of a higher order of nature than our own, against those who have power over the world in these dark days." St. Peter in his first sermon on Pentecost day said, "Repent, ask pardon of your sins, save yourself from this false minded generation."

Jesus Christ's mercy through the
Sacrament of Reconciliation

Divine mercy is there for the asking. We see how Jesus Christ was merciful to sinners and we have two great examples of Mary Magdalene and the Good Thief. God's mercy is given just as easily today, which can be obtained in confession. When we hear the words of absolution spoken by the priest, we have the assurance that our sins are forgiven. We know from experience that things do not bother us again after we go to confession - there is a reason for this. Confession also is a time when we can ask questions about our spiritual life, talk things over when we have a problem, and obtain spiritual direction.

Many wonder how often one should go to confession. I would suggest at least once a month. Vatican Council II urges frequent confession. It is a duty of the pastor to preach about frequent confession, and to be available for confession at all times. This is true for any priest. You have the right to receive the sacrament. Perhaps you do not have many sins. Still, you may come to confession. If you have very little to say, why not say, "Father, I am not aware of any mortal sins, but being human I must have sinned in some way, and I am sorry for whatever I have done wrong."

There is no reason why your confession should seem routine. If Father says you don't have to bother to come to confession for such minor things, tell him that you want to come and that it is your right to receive the sacrament. Don't let him brush you off.

I remember on one occasion a little girl said to me, "Father how would you like to go to confession?" We do go to confession - the Pope. Bishops, Priests, brothers and sisters go to confession.

In all the centuries great miracles of forgiveness of sins have occurred in the Christian confessional, where no one takes precedence over anyone else. Where all know their needs and find them answered over and over again. We learn also "To glorify God, Who has given such power to men."

IX - Prayer in Renewal of the Spiritual Life

Be Men of God

Vatican Council II wishes that we renew the inner man, that we change and become a new man. The most urgent thing in the plan of God today is that we be men of God. To become men of God, we have to be in contact with God. Many have lost this contact today, but if we are ever to bring the world to its senses we must become men of God. Thus, we must be men who speak to God, who hear God, who know God, and who experience God in our daily lives. It is not enough to believe in God. We must have deep convictions about God and the things of God. We may no longer keep God to ourselves, or sanctify ourselves alone. We need to have mutual confidence in one another. We must be willing to share our experiences with others. We should learn to be continually with God. We all have done or do many stupid things in our lives which could and should be cut out of our lives so that we are able to devote more time to God. Our best friend is God, and being with God in prayer is the best means of learning how to deal with the world and to live our own lives.

Prayer Life

Prayer is important in our life because it unites us to God so that we can give God to others. Prayer helps renew our spiritual life so that we can give spiritual life to all our activities. Prayer puts us in touch with God - We encounter God.

Formulated Prayer

First step - We use formulas, that is words written by others or by ourselves. We must remember that the value of prayer is not the words we say because God sees the heart. The words are only the occasion of our going to God. Our life must correspond with the words we say or we have a shallow and empty spiritual life. As we grow spiritually we do not need words any longer. They appear useless and sometimes even dangerous.

40

Second step - We do not use words which we used or were prepared before, that is exterior prayers. Words just do not appeal to us any longer. Rather, we feel a need to think about life in relation to God's will in our life. We want to know what God wants in our life. To use this form of prayer we need ideas to move our will. Thus it is good in the beginning to use a book, that is a spiritual book, or scripture. We call this form of prayer - Meditation. The value of meditation is not in the work of the intellect but in the will. The mind only formulates the ideas, but the will actually brings us in union with God in prayer. The use of mental pictures is helpful in meditation, but it is not essential. If we understand the part the intellect plays in this form of praying then we can use distractions and disturbances correctly.

Affective Prayer

Third Step - As we advance in prayer we notice that we will use our intellect less and less, and the will more and more Gradually the part the intellect plays is so reduced that we can say our prayer is really a prayer of the will. This is different in everyone of us, and it can be different every day in our prayer life. This form of prayer is called *Affective Prayer*. Affective signifies the will with something of the mind. We behold God and love Him. Thus, we use our mind and will in this form of prayer. We might think that our prayer is getting worse because we experience more distractions. Nevertheless the prayer we say is much better than what we had been saying, or practicing. Again we stress the value of our prayer is not a result of the exercise of the intellect, but a result of the exercise of the will. It would be useful to have a small booklet and write prayers in it to help us to begin our prayer. For example: "Stay with me Jesus," "Oh God I love you." Use any expression which might be useful.

Prayer of Simplicity

Fourth step - During this phase of praying, we will find that we no longer use the booklet. Why? Because the Holy Spirit works in us to use the same prayer over and over again. We might be using different words, but what we say

41

always has the same meaning. The Holy Spirit inspires and acts in us. This action of the Holy Spirit happens without our knowing it. A process of simplification takes place in our praying. This will happen if we are faithful to God. This form of prayer will lead to complete abandonment to God. We need to be generous in the beginning of our prayer life if we wish to arrive at this exalted state of prayer. If one makes the spiritual exercises of St. Ignatius with generosity, that is for a month, one should be able to arrive at this stage in one's spiritual development. It means that we have to give ourselves completely to God. Many never say that they give themselves completely to God, or if they do they do not mean it; therefore many are novices in prayer even fifty or sixty years later. We have to learn to live this prayer. This prayer is called the *prayer of simplicity*. Our life must be simple in living this form of prayer or our prayer life is not true.

The value of a prayerful person in the world cannot be imagined. Here is a new man - one identified with God. What will happen to such a person? A tremendous cross will be given such a person because the Holy Spirit desires more from him. The person asks how he can do more. He can do more if he continues to work with more difficulties. He will experience the Dark Night of the soul. It is easy to work with exterior difficulties. It is difficult to bear trials that affect one's personality. For example; a person has the temptation that his spiritual life is false, that he has wasted his time and his life, that what he has experienced is not from God. We have to encourage such a person. We have to tell him to be strong. It is the best time of his spiritual life.

Mystical Prayer

Fifth step - The spiritual life develops to such a point that a new contact with God begins. It is a passive mystical contact. The Holy Spirit begins to guide the soul and to teach what He wishes. When we have this form of prayer we recognize that God is working in our soul. Mystical prayer has more degrees than active prayer. Thus there will be a variety of experiences in the mystical state. The last degree of this form of prayer is when we are lived in completely by God. It is living the death. It means living in the awareness of the presence of God. This awareness of the presence of God can increase each day until we have the *transforming union* in which we can say in all truth,

"I live now not I but Christ lives in me."
"I must decrease, He must increase"

This is the type of prayer life we should try to develop. This is the renewal asked by Vatican Council II, and this is the renewed person the Apostolate of Christian Renewal hopes to produce.

X - Devotions and Renewal

The story if Fatima is known throughout the world, even if the majority of people ignore it. Throughout the years, revelations have been made by Our Lord and our Lady to Lucy, all of which are summed up in the title, "The Message of Fatima."

The message of Fatima stressed three things:

> Rosary - five decades to be said daily
> Reparation - by living the Christian life
> Consecration to the Immaculate Heart of Mary

Rosary

The request of reciting the rosary was not something new. Our Blessed Mother had already spoken at Lourdes about the need for this great prayer. She also stressed the need for reparation at Lourdes. Our Lord made known the need for atonement in the revelations at Paray-le-Monial, when He revealed the devotion to His Sacred Heart.

Immaculate Heart

What was new was the call for devotion to the Immaculate Heart of Mary and the Consecration to her Immaculate Heart. It was made known that it was the will of the Heavenly Father that all the world be consecrated to her Immaculate Heart.

In 1940, Lucy, at the command of her spiritual directors, wrote to Pope Pius XII asking for the consecration of the world to the Immaculate Heart of Mary, including the people of Russia in a special way.

On the last day of October, 1942, Pope Pius XII consecrated the Church and the world, including the people of Russia, to the Immaculate Heart of Mary. Our Lord made it known that this act of consecration was incomplete.

In May, 1948, Pope Pius XII issued an Encyclical to the world calling upon every family and every diocese to concur in this consecration.

July 7, 1962, Pope John XXIII instituted the Feast of Our Lady of the Rosary of Fatima.

November 21, 1964, Pope Paul VI renewed Pope Pius XII's consecration to the Immaculate Heart of Mary before the entire Eccumenical Council and simultaneously announced his own mission to Fatima.

May 13, 1965, Pope Paul VI, through a papal mission, presented a Golden Rose at Fatima, confiding the "Entire Church" to Mary's protection.

May 13, 1967, Pope Paul VI made a pilgrimage to Fatima proclaiming its message to the world.

Vatican Council II has upheld the position of honor of the Blessed Virgin Mary and her role in the Church (read Chapter VIII of the document *on the Church, Lumen Gentium*).

It is our desire to fulfill the will of the Heavenly Father in consecrating families to the Immaculate Heart of Mary; also to fulfill the requests of Our Blessed Mother and the urgings of the Holy Father, Pope Paul VI.

Having made the consecration to the Immaculate Heart of Mary, we urge all to live in such a way, that through her, peace may be granted to the world, that honor and glory be given to God, that families may be sanctified, that is, truly renewed, and that they may be formed in Christ.

The Rosary Devotion:

The Rosary is a prayer that can be said alone, but it is an ideal family prayer. As Father Peyton says, "The family that prays together stays together." We can say also that the family that prays together creates a better world.

The following are a few things we can meditate on while praying the rosary, and the virtues we can learn to practice.

The Joyful Mysteries

1. The Annunciation - Mary was still a very young virgin when the Archangel Gabriel came to her. Mary was not

45

expecting the angel. Rather, she was surprised and frightened at his greetings. This shows that she was humble - she was not expecting to be chosen to become the mother of the Messiah. The purity of Mary is shown in her answer, "How can this be since I know not man." When Mary knew the plan of God for her she believed. This immediate belief gives evidence of her strong faith. Her obedience followed immediately, "Let it be done to me according to your word." The Holy Spirit formed Christ in Mary only after she gave consent. He is to form Christ in us and He will do that only after we give our consent. Thus, we should be open to the Spirit as Mary was. We must be humble, pure, believing, and obedient.

2. The Visitation - Mary visited Elizabeth and conversed with her about the happenings in their lives because of God's designs. Mary's charity is shown in her coming to Elizabeth in time of need. She brought Christ with her as she always does. Elizabeth was moved by the Holy Spirit and acclaimed the greatness of Mary. Mary accepted the praise of Elizabeth, but rendered all honor and Glory to God who had done such great things for her, and in her. She is truly Blessed and all generations will think of her in this way. Besides the lessons of charity and humility we can learn from this mystery, I think that we can learn two other lessons. One is that when we are open to the Holy Spirit we will be able to recognize Christ in others. The second is that whenever Mary comes into our lives, she brings Christ with her. I think that we should, in a spirit of faith, invite Mary to come to us, to our families, to our friends and to the whole world. The blessings of Christ will be upon us.

Nativity - After Mary returned from visiting Elizabeth, St. Joseph wondered how Mary had become pregnant. He was going to put her away privately when the angel told him that her pregnancy had come through the power of the Most High. We need this testimony of St. Joseph to prove the virginity of Mary. He believed!

We see them go to Bethlehem to fulfill a civil decree, that is, to register in their own town. The lesson we can learn is that we are to obey all just civil laws. We can learn that God fulfills His plan through human happenings and events. The birth of Jesus took place in a cave. Thus, Christ immediately identified with the poor, and this was to be the pattern of His whole life.

Scripture relates the announcement of the birth of Christ to the Shepherds who are lowly people. They went in search of Christ and they found Him. Modern man is searching for God in his heart. He still is searching through emptyness so his heart is broken. There are many who are of good will. To these we should bring Christ.   ,

4. The Presentation - St. Joseph and Mary took Christ to the Temple. Simeon had been promised that he would see the Lord before he would die. He was moved by the Holy Spirit to come to the Temple on the day of the Christ Child's presentation, and when he saw Christ, whom he recognized to be the Messiah, Simeon received Christ in his arms and predicted the sufferings of Christ and of Mary. God did not spare His own Son, nor did He spare Mary. They suffered for others, for us. We can learn much about the value of suffering, and the place of suffering in the spiritual life if we meditate on this correctly. Suffering in the spiritual life can be a blessing or a curse. What it is depends on each one of us.

Again the lesson of being open to the Spirit is given to us. The Spirit will move us to go to Church where we will find Christ in the Blessed Sacrament of the Altar.

5. Finding of Christ in the Temple - We see the search of St. Joseph and Mary for Christ and we witness their finding of Him amid the learned Doctors of the law. The Doctors were amazed at the knowledge of Christ - a twelve-year-old-boy. Mary asked Him why He had acted as He did. His answer was that He had to be about His Father's business. Christ was not really lost since He was in His Father's House. We see from Christ's answer that He knew His mission in life. Scripture tells us that Mary kept all these things in her heart, and that Christ went home with Mary and Joseph and was obedient to them.

God is not dead as was believed in the 1960's. He is just a hidden God, and all who seek Him will find Him. Where? They should find Him in us and we should lead them back to their Father's House where they will find the real Christ.

47

The Sorrowful Mysteries

1. The Agony in the Garden - Christ prayed to the Father to remove this Chalice of suffering from Him if that were possible, but He always said, "Not my will but Thine be done." We can think about the interior sufferings of Christ; His invitation to the Apostles to pray with Him and their reaction; His arrest and the incidents that took place at that time.

2. The scourging at the Pillar - we can meditate on what happened after the arrest; His imprisonment, His trial up to that point; the scourging and the exterior sufferings He endured from that form of punishment.

3. The Crowning with Thorns - We can meditate on the things that happened before He was crowned with thorns, and when Pilate exclaimed, "Behold the Man." We can meditate on the actual sufferings of Christ, standing before the people, being treated as a criminal; the derision and insults hurled at Him, and the cry for His crucifixion.

4. The Carrying of the Cross - Think about the remainder of the trial. His sentence to death. His way of the cross in detail, especially meeting His mother, being stripped of His garments, and the nailing to the Cross.

5. The Crucifixion - The suffering of Christ on the cross, the things He said, especially the giving of us to Mary as her children, and the giving of her to us as our mother; His death, the piercing of His side with a lance, and His burial.

At this point of our meditation we can unite ourselves with the consecration at each Mass being celebrated throughout the world.

The sorrowful mysteries teach us much about suffering and love; for no greater love can a man have than to give his life for his friends.

The Glorious Mysteries

1. The Resurrection - Christ rises from the dead. We can visualize the appearance of Christ to the Apostles, the disciples, and to others; the things He says and does - especially the giving of the power to forgive sin, and the encounter with Peter. We can meditate on what the resurrec-

tion of Christ means to us - the victory over death, over sin, and an assurance of our own resurrection. The resurrection of Christ proves that He was divine - that He is God.

2. The Ascension - Think about Christ's last words to the Apostles; His promise of sending the Holy Spirit; His ascent into heaven to be at the right hand of His Father in glory; the angels telling the apostles to go about their business because Christ will come again.

3. The Descent of the Holy Spirit - We can meditate on the gathering of the Apostles with Mary and the others in the upper room to pray for the coming of the Holy Spirit; the coming of the Holy Spirit and the effects of His coming upon the Apostles; the activities of the Apostles immediately after the coming of the Holy Spirit. We should ask the Holy Spirit to come to us, and to form Christ in us. We can make a spiritual communion at this time in union with all masses said throughout the world.

4. The Assumption of the Blessed Mother into Heaven - We should think about the life of Mary before her death, that is, from the time of the crucifixion until her death; her assumption into heaven, body and soul; her entrance into glory and eternal happiness.

5. Crowning of the Blessed Virgin in Heaven - The Blessed Virgin Mary, the Mother of God, Mother of Christ - the God-man, Mother of the Church, Mother of men, is crowned the Queen of Heaven and earth, the Queen of angels and of men.

There are many ways in which we can pray the rosary so that it will never be boring or meaningless. Some like to think about the words they say; others like to meditate on the mysteries, or read some thoughts before each mystery, or read a short saying before each Hail Mary. No matter - if it is done correctly, it is a great benefit to one's spiritual life and personal renewal. It is also beneficial for family renewal.

The Enthronement of the Sacred Heart in the Home

Jesus Christ wishes to share His love with us in our home, and since our home is a domestic Church we should invite Him to come into our home through the Enthronement of the Sacred Heart.

Enthronement of the Sacred Heart

The enthronement of the Sacred Heart in the home is a crusade to the whole world to the love of the Sacred Heart. It is an act of solemn, royal homage that is offered to the Sacred Heart, the King of Kings, Lord of the world. At the same time, it is a solemn social recognition of the Kingship of the Sacred Heart of Jesus over our home, over society, over the country; and an act of social reparation for all modern refusals to accept His Kingship, as shamelessly flaunted in godless legislation, godless schools, godless families. In opposition to such acts of "de-enthronment," we freely choose to enthrone Our King.

Love

The core, the heart, the essence of the Enthronement is bound up in one word - *love*. It strives to bring into the hearts of men full realization of the love of the Sacred Heart for them.

In order to accomplish this, the enthronement calls for an active spiritual program of three points: prayer, the Eucharist and penance.

Prayer

We have already said much about prayer since it is necessary for salvation, for renewal, and for spiritual growth. The enthronement stresses a life of love, which will make prayer easy and familiar. We pray as we love; prayer is simply an "Exchange of love." The prayer we are speaking about in the enthronement is family prayer. There was a time when family prayer was common; the enthronement strives to make it so again. Thus we strongly urge family prayer. There are different forms of family prayer which are recommended.

The Family Rosary.

Shared prayer - Begin the prayer with a song, then anyone who feels like praying a personal prayer should do so. The others are to listen, trying to make this prayer their own. They are not to interrupt or question what is being said. They are not even to discuss what was said during this prayer meeting. After the first one finishes, the next one may express his prayer in like manner. This continues until everyone who wishes to pray out loud has had an opportunity to do so. At first, you will find much hesitation because no one is used to praying like this. Moments of silence, even long periods of silence are acceptable. The more one prays in this manner the more one will enjoy it and the more he will gain from it. One must always keep in mind, that "when two or three are gathered in Christ's name," there God is in the midst of them. The shared prayer session is finished with a song.

Scriptural reading and shared prayer - Sing a song, read a passage from scripture, think about it awhile, then say what the passage means to you. Again do not ask questions, interrupt, or speak about it after the session is over. After everyone has had an opportunity to say what he thinks, turn these thoughts shared into prayer as described above.

For daily family praying, you can also use the prayers in the Booklet called, "Family Prayer Renewal of the Heart of Christ" (Blue Booklet) and the "Holy Hour Booklet" (Green). These two booklets have become popular for family praying in the United States. They can be obtained from the National Center of the Enthronement, 3 Adams Street, Fairhaven, Mass. 02719.

In frequent family gatherings for prayer, the King of Love becomes a living member of the family. He shares in all the joyful and sorrowful happenings in the home, and by His constant presence in the family produces that peace which is the source of Christian happiness.

Family Holy Hour is designed to make reparation in a spirit of generous love and penance for the fatal modern social apostasy of the home; for the sins of pride and sensuality of so many so-called "Christian" families. This holy

51

hour should be made once a week, or at least once a month. It can be made together in a family group, or individually. It is to be made between the hours of nine in the evening and six in the morning.

Father Mateo, the founder of the enthronement in the home, urges the night adorers to begin their holy hour by uniting themselves with all the priests who at that moment are offering the Holy Sacrifice of the Mass in some part of the world. He suggests that they pray for the following intentions: For the Holy Father, for the clergy, for those who have gone astray, for the dying, for peace, for the social reign of the Sacred Heart especially through the enthronement.

The Eucharist

The Enthronement seeks to make the home a Eucharistic Tabernacle. It calls for frequent, even daily assistance at Mass and the reception of Holy Communion. The home thus becomes a Eucharistic shrine, a genuine Christian sanctuary filled with the presence of Our Lord, for the members, living the Mass in their daily lives, bring the Fount of Grace which they receive in Holy Communion immediately into the home, to remain there while they live the Christian life. The enthronement of the image of the Sacred Heart is a constant reminder of the abiding presence of Christ. The two tabernacles of the Church and the home are united by the common bond of the Sacred Heart of Jesus.

Penance

The third part of the enthronement, penance, is perhaps the most difficult because it calls for Christian action. This is the doctrine of the Cross. Before Our Lord chose the cross as an instrument of redemption, it was universally held as an abomination. It was shunned, despised, rated the object of intense shame and infamy. But Jesus, in dying on the cross sanctified it, enobled it, and raised it to the sublime heights of eternal glory.

Christian Doctrine is this, that men share in the passion, the Cross of Christ, by their own individual sufferings, misfortunes, sorrows and mortifications. They share in the Cross if they accept these ills in the proper spirit and offer them as a sacrifice which contributes to the salvation of souls.

The enthronement of the Sacred Heart of Jesus in the home has a certain religious ceremony to initiate and stimulate its program. There are definite acts of what may be called devotion. These are helps. They are good, even in themselves. They are important, but in themselves they are not the enthronement.

In the most central part of the home, usually the living room, a table is arranged like an altar, with candles, flowers, and other suitable decorations. An image of the Sacred Heart (picture or statue) is placed on a table nearby with holy water. Guests have been invited, and the family is present if possible. The pastor, or assistant priest, has been invited to preside.

Vatican Council II, in the decree on the Apostolate of the Laity, stated: "The family has received from God its mission to be the first vital cell of society. It will fulfill this mission if the whole family is caught up in the liturgical worship of the Church."

And Pope Paul wrote, "Where, in fact, apart from churches and oratories, is the Divine Heart of Jesus more fittingly adored than in the sanctuary of the family. If the cult of the Sacred Heart of Jesus, King and friend of the family, is thus nourished by liturgical worship, especially in the Holy Sacrifice of the Mass, personal and family devotion of the Sacred Heart (will become) a witness to the true faith, to sincere love."

This is the reason we have combined Mass in the home with the enthronement of the Sacred Heart. The Eucharist was established in a private home, the Cenacle. What better place then, other than a parish church, of course, is there in which to celebrate the Eucharistic sacrifice than in the "Domestic Sanctuary" of the home? These masses of the enthronement instruct the People of God in the true meaning of the Mass, sanctify the family through the presence of Christ and His priest, and increase daily mass attendance. When combined with the Sacred Heart enthronement the stress is on the heart of the Mass - the Love of Jesus; His loving person; His abiding presence in the home through the Enthronement and through continued family prayer.

Guidelines of the Apostolate of Christian Renewal
Purpose:

1. To give honor and glory to God.
2. To sanctify one's own soul and to help sanctify others.
3. To be of service to those in need.
4. To make prayerful intercession for the Holy Father, the bishop or bishops in one's diocese, one's pastor, associate pastors, religious working in the parish, and for the people of God within the parish.
5. To pray especially for priests, brothers, sisters who may have a crisis in their vocation, faith, or in any other area.
6. To pray for those priests, brothers, and sisters who have left their calling and returned to live in the world.
7. To make reparation to the Sacred Heart of Jesus through the Immaculate and Sorrowful Heart of Mary for the sins of the whole world.
8. To spread devotion to the Sacred Heart of Jesus and the Immaculate Heart of Mary.

Spiritual Exercises

These prayers are *only suggestions and do not bind under sin —*

1. Daily Prayers:
   a) Fifteen minutes of meditation.
   b) Mystical Mass prayer.
   c. Chaplet Rosary of the Holy Spirit.
   d) Recitation of the Rosary (with the family when possible).
   e) Renewal of Consecration to Jesus Christ through Mary.
   f) Renewal prayer of the Enthronement of the Sacred Heart and the Consecration to the Immaculate Heart of Mary.
2. If possible, daily Mass, offered in the spirit of reparation.
3. Holy hour in the home once a week (or at least once a month)between the hours of 9:00 P.M. to 6:00 A.M.
4. As a sign of one's consecration, wear the Brown Scapular of Our Lady of Mount Carmel, or the Scapular medal.

5. Make a retreat once a year.
6. If possible, a visit to the Blessed Sacrament daily for a five minute retreat.

Works to be fostered:

1. Foster fidelity to the faith, loyalty to the Holy Father, obedience to the Magisterium, that is the Pope and the bishops as described in the documents of Vatican Council II.
2: Encourage the Enthronement of the Sacred Heart in the home (with mass in the home wherever possible) ; Night adoration in the home in a spirit of reparation for the sins of the world; First Friday devotion .
3. Encourage the consecration of the family to the Immaculate Heart of Mary. Also encourage the family rosary, First Saturday devotions, Eucharistic reparation; the wearing of the Scapular of Carmel or the Medal.
4. Encourage others to recite the Chaplet Rosary of the Holy Spirit.
5. Become involved in service to those in need, that is, helping the poor, the underprivileged, the sick, orphans, prisoners, the aged.

Organizations

1. You may join as an individual without forming a group.
2. You may form a group within your own parish; then, you would be a leader. Remember, a real leader gets others involved and gives them responsibility.
3. Send the names of those who make the consecration to the National Director.
4. Give a report once a year of accomplishments in service to others of the manner in which community is being formed in the parish, or diocese, or civic community. This report is to be sent to the National Director.

Finances:

1. There will be no fees or dues.
2. Each member will pay for his own books, booklets, news letter, or religious supplies.
3. Any donation you wish to send to the National Director to carry on the work of the apostolate will be greatly appreciated.

Preparation before joining the Apostolate of

Christian Renewal

In order to become a member of the Apostolate of Christian Renewal we ask each one to make a consecration to Mary, to renew his or her baptismal vows, and to make a total commitment to Jesus Christ.

We ask each one to make a four week preparation before joining the Apostolate because it is a serious step. We do not want it to be something which is just emotional. We do not want people to join just for the sake of joining. The Apostolate is something to be lived. It is a commitment to become aware of what took place at our baptism, and confirmation and to live that life with zeal and love. We are actually making a covenant with God. We are saying, "We are your children and you are our God."

Suggested prayers during the time of Preparation.

1. Daily Mass
2. Daily Rosary
3. Chaplet of the Holy Spirit
4. Meditation on the following:

First Week — Knowledge of Self

1st day "God saw that all He had made was very good." (Gen. 1:31)
God said, "Let us make mankind in our own image and likeness; and let them have dominion over the fish of the sea, the birds of the air, the cattle; over all the wild animals and every creature that crawls on earth" (Gen. 1:26) God created us a little less than the angels; in His image and likeness; as King and master of the whole world. Therefore, we are greater than the whole world. He did this because of love.

2nd day When we were baptized we became a supernatural person; that is we became participators in the very life of God. We became members of the family of God. We become children of the Father; brothers of Christ, and Temples of the Holy Spirit. Therefore, we are brothers and sisters of each other. Everyone is our brother or sister in Christ

3rd day Our Father in Heaven should be able to say - "You are my beloved son in whom I am well pleased." "You are my beloved daughter in whom I am well pleased."

4th day To become a beloved son or daughter we have to put on Christ.
We should compare ourselves with Christ and no one else; therefore do not judge others. (Mt. 7/15)
"I greatly admire Christ. I could easily be His follower, but I have never met a true Christian" Mahatma Gandhi
"Am I a true Christian - an Apostle?"

5th day An Apostle is a committed person
Commitment means to give oneself. It is a total gift that expresses the past, present, and future. It is a mystery which can only come from within oneself. This responsibility I can not pass on to anyone else.
You need not fear that you are unworthy to make a commitment. No one is ever worthy! *God chooses us first.*
As a truly committed person I can affect the well-being of the whole world!

6th day "The reason why Christianity has not succeeded is because it has never been tried." Chesterton.
"You are the salt of the earth; but if the salt loses its strength, what shall it be salted with? It is no longer of any use but to be thrown out and trodden underfoot by men."
"You are the light of the world. A city set on a mountain cannot be hidden. Neither do men light a lamp and put it under a measure, but upon the lampstand, so as to give light to all in the house. Even so let your light shine before men that they may see your good works and give glory to your Father in Heaven." (Mt. 5 : 13-16)

7th day If we try to renew ourselves and become followers of Christ and live the life of a true Christian, we will have to carry the cross.
"If the world hates you, know that it has hated me before you. If you were of the world, the world

57

would love what is its own. But because you are not of the world, therefore the world hates you. Remember the word I have spoken to you: No servant is greater than his master. If they have persecuted me, they will persecute you also; If they have kept my word, they will keep yours also." Jn. 15:18 If we remain united to Christ we will bear much fruit.

"Abide in Me, and I in you. As a branch cannot bear fruit of itself unless it remain on the vine, so neither can you unless you abide in Me. I am the vine; you are the branches. He who abides in me, and I in Him, he bears much fruit; for without me you can do nothing." Jn. 15: 4-5

Second Week — Knowledge of the World

1st day "Thou shalt love the Lord your God with your whole heart and with your whole soul and with your whole mind - This is the greatest and the first commandment. And the second is like it: You shall love your neighbor as yourself." Mt. 22/29-37; Mk. 12/30-31

Everyone is my neighbor and brother! Lk. 10/29-37 Love of neighbor as yourself asks much —
— I will not deny anyone what I give to myself
— this love eliminates all negative attitudes towards others.
it is the beginning of the practice of justice.
It means to keep the commandments of God. If we do this we show great service to our neighbor.

2nd day On another occasion Christ said that we should love our neighbor as we love Him.
— to love in this manner, we will put the positive blue-print of Christian living into practice, that is we will live the beatitudes.

3rd day At the Last Supper, Christ washed the feet of the Apostles and said, "This is My Commandment - that you love one another as I love you. Jn. 13/34-35
Greater love than this no one has, that one lay down his life for his friends." Jn. 15/14

58

If we love our neighbor as Christ loves us, we are asking Him to love through us without blocking Him with ourselves.

"I live now, not I, but Christ lives in me."

4th day   The summit of Christian love must be a mutual love in imitation of the Blessed Trinity in loving. Only Christianity has dared to demand such heights of love — to love with the love of God!

Begin on earth to love and imitate the life of the Blessed Trinity. This love leads to the conversion of the world.

Whoever has a heart full of love always has something to give. *That means you.*

5th day   Love of God and neighbor must be positive and show forth in our daily lives. We do this by following the blue-print of Christian living; living the beatitudes preached by Christ in the Sermon of the Mount. Mt. 5 : 3-12.

Blessed are the poor in spirit - the meek - those who mourn - who hunger and thirst for justice - the merciful - the pure of heart - the peacemakers - those who suffer persecution for justice's sake - when men reproach you and persecute you -

— In living the beatitudes we also carry out the practice of the corporal and spiritual works of mercy.

Corporal Works of Mercy: Feed the hungry; give drink to the thirsty; clothe the naked; visit the imprisoned; shelter the homeless; visit the sick; bury the dead.

Spiritual Works of Mercy: Admonish the sinner; instruct the ignorant; counsel the doubtful; comfort the sorrowful; bear wounds patiently; forgive all injuries; pray for the living and the dead. The world is a vast hospital. We see the broken-hearted everywhere. Let us help them.

6th day   "Amen, I say to you, as long as you did it for one of these, the least of my brethern, you did it for me" Mt. 25 :40.

As a *child* of God *you* are the hope of the world!
Something to marvel at! The world needs you,
your talents, prayers and sacrifices.

7th day "Let him who is greatest among you become as
the least, and him who is the chief become as the
servant" Lk. 22:26

Let us rejoice with those who do good, and have
compassion on those who do evil.

"You have heard that it was said: 'Thou shalt love
thy neighbor, and shall hate thy enemy.' But I say
to you, love your enemies, do good to those who
hate you, and pray for those who persecute and
calumniate you. Thus, you will be children of your
Father in heaven, who makes His sun to rise on
the good and the evil, and sends rain on the just
and the unjust." Mt. 5:43-45, Lk. 6:27-38

Third Week — Knowledge of Mary, Our Mother

1st day A young mother of 15 or 16 years of age is chosen
to be the mother of Jesus.

"Hail, Full of grace, the Lord is with thee. Blessed
are Thou among women." Lk. 1:28

— at Lourdes, Mary said, "I am the Immaculate
Conception.

". . .and behold, thou shalt conceive in thy womb
and bring forth a son. . ." Lk. 1:31

"How shall this happen, since I do not know man?"
Lk. 1:34

"The Holy Spirit shall come upon you and the
power of the Most High shall overshadow thee"
Lk. 1:35

"Behold the handmaid of the Lord; be it done to
me according to Thy word." Lk. 1:38

The Holy Spirit formed Christ in Mary after she
gave her consent. He will form Christ in us only
after we give Him our consent.

2nd day Elizabeth filled with the Holy Spirit said: "Blessed are you among women and blessed is the
fruit of your womb! And how have I deserved that
the mother of my Lord come to me? For behold,
the moment that the sound of thy greeting came

to my ears, the babe in my womb leapt for joy. And blessed is she who believed, because the things promised her by the Lord shall be accomplished." (Lk. 1:42-45)

Mary could not keep her secret. Elizabeth recognized Christ in Mary through the inspiration of the Holy Spirit.

— Mary always brings Christ with her

— We will recognize Christ in her and in others through the inspiration of the Holy Spirit. Thus, the importance of being close to and open to the Holy Spirit.

3rd day Mary's reaction to Elizabeth's praise was one of humility. She recognized the gifts from God, and thanked Him for what He had done for her.

Read the Magnificat — Lk. 1: 46-55

We should look into our lives and realize the many gifts, talents, and assets God has given to us. Let us be grateful, joyful, and peaceful.

4th day Christ is born in poverty - the Holy Family can identify themselves with the poor.

The angels sang - "Glory to God in the highest, and peace on earth among men of good will." Lk. 2:14

Modern man is searching for the God of his heart but often he searches through emptiness therefore he has a broken heart.

Many are men of good will. We must bring Christ to them. The Holy Spirit will help them to recognize Christ.

Let each one of us be open to the Holy Spirit and help others to be open to Him.

5th day "And thy own soul a sword shall pierce, that the thoughts of many hearts may be revealed."

Mary was to suffer for the good of others. Christ did not spare His own mother from sufferings. Suffering has a place in salvation history.

What do I think about suffering? How do I accept it in my own life, in the life of my family, relatives, friends, world?

61

6th day Loss of Christ in the temple. After finding him, Mary said: "Son, why have you done so to us? Behold thy Father and I have been seeking you sorrowing" (Lk. 2:48)

— "How is it that you sought me? Did you not know that I must be about My Father's business?" Modern man has lost Christ. He will have to seek Him again.

Where will he find Him? He should be able to find Him in *You*. A true Christian!

You must lead others back to Christ's Father's House where they will find the real Christ - in the Blessed Sacrament.

God is not dead as believed in the 1960's; He is hidden, yet those who seek Him will find Him. The 1970's are waiting for the resurrected God! Will you help others to find Christ?

7th day At the wedding Feast of Cana, Mary said, "Do what He tells you." And the water was changed into wine.

At the Crucifixion, Mary watched her Son die.

"Son behold thy mother; Mother behold thy son." Mary is our mother and she loves us dearly. She brings Christ to us and brings us to Christ.

We must live the Rosary - pray the rosary - meditate on the mysteries of the rosary. Through the rosary we will learn much about our faith.

We should make a consecration to the Immaculate and Sorrowful Heart of Mary - then live it!

Fourth Week — Knowledge of Jesus Christ,

Our God and Brother.

1st day Let us call to mind the mystery of the Incarnation The Second Person of the Blessed Trinity assumed a human nature from the Blessed Virgin Mary

Therefore, in Christ there are two natures: One Divine; the other human. But there is only one Person - a Divine Person.

Therefore, Christ is God and Man.

62

2nd day At Christ's baptism the Heavenly Father said: "This is my Beloved Son in Whom I am well pleased." Lk. 3:22

Who is Christ?

a) "Who do people say the Son of Man is?" Mt. 16:13

— John the Baptist, Eliah, Jeremiah or one of the prophets (Mt. 16:14)

b) "Who do you say I am?" Mt. 16:15

Simon Peter's answer - "You are the Messiah, the Son of the Living God." Mt. 16:17

c) "Blessed are you, Simon-bar-Jona, for flesh and blood has not revealed this to you but My Father who is in Heaven." Mt. 16:17

3rd day Christ was also a true man.

Christ was a true man. He lived as a man, feasted as a man with the common people at wedding celebrations. He suffered fatigue and hunger.

His own townsmen said of Him: "Is not this the carpenter's son?"

The moral character of Christ was beyond reproach and He revealed the tender nature of His heart throughout His life. He was kind, compassionate, and understanding of other people's pains and problems.

Christ was a man for others. He became a true victim.

4th day The mission of Christ.

His mission was to save others by dying on the cross; to take our sins upon Himself.

He knew how He would die - on the cross; when He would die; how much and what suffering He would have to undergo. He predicted His own death.

The vocation of Christ was to carry the burdens of man within His heart. We can readily imagine the inner sufferings of Christ which He bore all his life as a foretaste of His passion. His inner feelings and sufferings were openly expressed in the Garden of Gethsemane. Lk. 22:43

His mission was to be carried out down through the centuries, and to the whole world.

5th day Christ established His Church, which is a gift of the Divine love of His Sacred Heart through the coming of the Holy Spirit.

— Christ established a hierarchical church, not a democratic church.

— Peter was chosen by the Father to be the Head of the Church - since He revealed to Peter who Christ was.

— Then Christ said: "And I say to you, you are Peter, and upon this rock I will build My Church, and the gates of hell shall not prevail against it."

— Peter was far from a rock. Therefore, Christ was referring to the Primacy of Peter.

— The Pope is the true successor of Peter, and the bishops of the apostles.

— Love the Pope, the bishops, priests, religious and pray for them.

6th day The Mission of the Church.

"Go, therefore, and make disciples of all nations, baptizing them in the name of the Father, and of the Son, and of the Holy Spirit, *teaching* them to *observe all* that I have commanded you; and behold, I am with you all days, even unto the consummation of the world.

— You are the Church. Therefore, you have to preach Christ and His message. You also have to live His Message!

— Remember, you are what you are in the sight of God; nothing more and nothing less!

— In order to live His message, you should make a total commitment to Christ; making a covenant with Him. This should be done also in your family circle, in your domestic Church, which is your home by having the Enthronement of the Sacred Heart of Jesus.

7th day A Committed Christian loves His Church, upholds the faith as taught by the Church, and does everything he can to spread the message of Christ.

— He lives his faith by going to the sacraments, by praying, by giving loving service to his neighbor.

— Remember, you will learn more about your total commitment through living the Christian life.

— Let this be our motto: Lord, Give me the serenity to accept the things I cannot change (other people's minds and personality) - Your Territory! The courage to change the things I can (My own weaknesses, faults, and failings) My Territory! The wisdom to know the difference. (Between Your Territory and Mine.)

Ceremony for the Total Commitment to Jesus Christ
Through the Blessed Virgin Mary (without Mass)

1. Hymn suitable for the occasion.

2. Talk by the priest or the one presiding.

3. Offering of the consecrants:
   Father, I present the following consecrants to be en-
   rolled in the Apostolate of Christian Renewal...

4. Suitable Hymn

5. Consecrants read the prayer of commitment:

   In the presence of the heavenly court, I, N........, choose
   you today as my mother. I deliver and consecrate myself to you completely; my body and soul, my goods,
   both interior and exterior, and even the value of all
   my good actions, past, present, and future.

   I also renew and ratify today in your hands, O Immaculate Mother, the vows of my baptism; I renounce
   forever Satan, his pomps and works.

   Through your hands, O Blessed Mother, I consecrate
   and commit myself entirely to Jesus Christ, your Son
   and my Brother, to carry my cross after Him all the
   days of my life, and to be more faithful to Him than
   ever before.

   Grant that I may be faithful in living this commit-
   every day of my life. **Amen.**

6. The one presiding:

   My brothers and sisters, may Almighty God bless
   you and keep you faithful to your commitment to Jesus
   through Mary.

Ceremony for the Total Commitment to Jesus Christ Through the Blessed Virgin Mary (with the Mass)

1. Entrance Song.
2. Greeting prayer, Penitential Rite, Litany of Mercy.
3. Glory to God.
4. First Scriptural Reading and Response.
5. Second Scriptural Reading and Gospel Acclamation.
6. Gospel.
7. Homily.
8. Creed (if no creed, the Apostles' Creed).
9. Prayer of intercession.
10. Offertory Hymn and Procession.
11. Commitment Ceremony:

    In the presence of the heavenly court, I N...., choose you today as my mother. I deliver and consecrate myself to you completely; my body and soul, my goods, both interior and exterior, and even the value of all my good actions, past, present, and future.

    I also renew and ratify today in your hands, O Immaculate Mother, the vows of my baptism; I renounce forever Satan, his pomps and works.

    Through your hands, O Blessed Mother, I consecrate and commit myself entirely to Jesus Christ, your Son and my Brother, to carry my cross after Him all the days of my life, and to be more faithful to Him than ever before.

    Grant that I may be faithful in living my commitment every day of my life. Amen.

13. Communion Hymn.
14. Priest presiding says:

    My brothers and sisters, may Almighty God bless you and keep you faithful to your commitment to Jesus through Mary.

15. Finish the Mass.
16. Suitable Hymn.

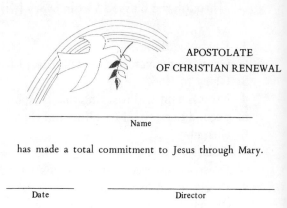

APOSTOLATE
OF CHRISTIAN RENEWAL

_____
Name

has made a total commitment to Jesus through Mary.

_____   _____
Date   Director

FOR FAMILIES

Consecration of the Family to the Immaculate Heart of Mary

Blessing of the Home

Priest: Peace be to this house.

R.   Sprinkle me, O Lord, with hyssop, and I shall be purified; wash me and I shall be whiter than snow. Have mercy on me, O Lord, in your mercy. Glory be to the Father and to the Son and to the Holy Spirit.

R.   As it was in the beginning, is now, and ever shall be, world without end. Amen.

Priest: Sprinkle me, O Lord with hyssop, and I shall be purified; wash me and I shall be whiter than snow. V. O Lord, hear my prayer. R. And let my cry come to you. V. The Lord be with you. R. And also with you.

Let us pray:

Hear us, Lord, Holy Father, almighty and eternal God, and graciously send your holy angel from heaven to watch over, to cherish, to protect, to abide with, and to defend all who dwell in this house. Through Christ Our Lord. R. Amen.

Solemn Blessing of the image of the Blessed Virgin Mary

P.   Our help is in the name of the Lord.

All. Who made heaven and earth.

P.   The Lord be with you.

All. And also with you.

Let us pray:

Almighty and everlasting God, you do not forbid us to carve or paint likenesses of your saints, in order that whenever we look at them with our bodily eyes we may call to mind their holy lives, and resolve to follow in their footsteps; may it please You to bless and to hallow this statue (or picture), which has been made in memory and honor of the Blessed Virgin Mary, Mother of Our Lord Jesus Christ, and grant that all who in its presence pay devout homage to the

69

Blessed Virgin may by her merits and intercession obtain your grace in this life and everlasting glory in the life to come, through Christ our Lord.

All: Amen.

The image is sprinkled with holy water (Roman Ritual).

Act of Consecration of the family to the Immaculate Heart of Mary (Begun by father or mother, said by all)

Queen of the Most Holy Rosary, and tender Mother of men,/ to fulfill the desires of the Sacred Heart,/ and the request of the Vicar of your Son on earth,/ we consecrate ourselves to you, and to your Immaculate Heart,/ and recommend to you,/ all the families of our nation, and the world.

Please accept our consecration, dearest Mother,/ and use us and all families as you wish,/ to accomplish your designs upon the world.

O Immaculate Heart of Mary,/ Queen of heaven and earth, and of our family,/ rule over us, together with the Sacred Heart of Jesus Christ, Our King.

Save us from the spreading flood of modern paganism,/ kindle in our hearts and homes the love of purity,/ the practice of the Christian life, and an ardent zeal for souls, and for the holiness of family life.

We come with confidence to you,/ O Throne of Grace and Mother of Fair Love;/ inflame us with the same divine fire which has inflamed your own Immaculate Heart.

Make our hearts and homes your shrine,/ and through us make the Heart of Jesus / rule and triumph in every family in the world. Amen.

Our Father, Hail Mary, Glory Be — for the intentions of the Holy Father.

All: Hail, Queen and Mother of mercy, hail, our life, comfort, and hope. Exiled sons of Eve, with loud voice we call upon you. As we journey in sorrow and lament through this valley of tears, we sigh and long for your help. Come then, our advocate, and turn those eyes of pity toward us now. When this time of exile is past, show us Jesus, the blessed Fruit of your womb, gentle, loving and kind Virgin Mary.

P.   Pray for us, Holy Mother of God.

All. Make us worthy of the promises of Christ.

Enthronement of the Sacred Heard of Jesus in the home
(with Mass in the home)

Entrance Hymn

Petitions (By Celebrant) :
1. For all the times we have failed to recognize Christ as the head of our families. All: Lord, have mercy.
2. For all the times we have hurt one another with our words and acts. All: Lord, have mercy.
3. For all the times we have refused to forgive those who have offended us. All: Lord, have mercy.
4. For all the times we have been selfish and inconsiderate of others. All: Christ, have mercy.
5. For all the times we have given bad example to our neighbors. All: Christ, have mercy.
6. For all the times we have failed to see Christ in one another. All: Christ, have mercy.
7. For all the times we have been lazy in performing our duties. All: Lord, have mercy.
8. For all the times we have spoken uncharitably about others. All: Lord, have mercy.
9. For all the times we have lacked the courage to be truly committed Christians. All: Lord, have mercy.

Gloria

First Scriptural reading : 1 John 4 : 7-12

Scriptural responses : (Gradual)

Gospel : Mt. 11 : 25-30

Homily

Enthronement ceremony after the Homily — *Blessing of the Image* —held by the father of the family.

Priest : Our help is in the name of the Lord

All : Who made heaven and earth

Priest : The Lord be with you

All : And also with you

Priest : Let us pray :

Almighty, everlasting God, who approves the painting and sculpturing of the images of your saints, so that as often as we gaze upon them we are reminded to imitate their deeds, bless and sanctify this image made in honor and in memory

71

of the most Sacred Heart of your only begotten Son, Our Lord Jesus Christ; and grant that whoever in its presence humbly strives to serve and honor the Sacred Heart of your only begotten Son, may obtain through His merits and intercession grace in this life and everlasting glory in the world to come. Amen.

(Image is sprinkled with holy water.)

Enthronement of the image by the father of the family.

(If possible, the picture or statue of the Sacred Heart should be enthroned in back of the altar, which is facing the people, so that all can see during the mass. Otherwise in a conspicious place.

Creed — If the creed is not said during the Mass, all now recite the Apostles' Creed as an act of faith and reparation.

The Apostles' Creed

I believe in God, the Father Almighty, Creator of heaven and earth; and in Jesus Christ, His only Son, our Lord; who was conceived by the Holy Spirit, born of the Virgin Mary, suffered under Pontius Pilate, was crucified, died and was buried. He descended into hell; the third day He rose again from the dead. He ascended into heaven, sits at the right hand of God, the Father Almighty; from there He shall come to judge the living and the dead.

I believe in the Holy Spirit, the Holy Catholic Church, the communion of Saints, the forgiveness of sins, the resurrection of the body and life everlasting. Amen.

Act of Consecration as Follows:

Almighty and Eternal Father, we the .... family (each member of the family says his first name beginning with the father) consecrate ourselves and our home to the Sacred Heart of your only begotten Son who loves us with a tender and everlasting love. May we return this love as He comes into the midst of our family to live and share our life in a special way from this day on.

We accept you, Divine Heart of Jesus, as our loving King and as a member of this family. Stay with us, Lord. Sanctify our joys and comfort us in all our sorrows. May your Holy Spirit penetrate each of us that we may be continually aware of Your special presence among us, especially in one another. Help us through this consecration to have a deep and loving respect for one another so that we may daily live this consecration in our family life.

Let our love go beyond our home into the world so that we may do our part to win other families to your Sacred Heart; thus helping to form a real community among the families of this parish and of the whole world.

All. Sacred Heart of Jesus, we love you.
Sacred Heart of Jesus, Thy kingdom come!
Immaculate Heart of Mary, pray for us.
St. Joseph, pray for us.
St. Margaret Mary, pray for us.
Glory to the Sacred Heart of Jesus forever and ever.
Amen.

Covenant — Signing the Certificate by the father, mother, and children (the priest signs at the end of the Mass)

Suggested Prayer of Intercession:

Introductory prayer (Celebrant):

Lord Jesus, You have told us, "Whatever you ask the Father in My name, He will give it to you," grant this family the petitions which they are about to present to Your Father in Your name.

Father:

That the Sacred Heart of Jesus may be known and loved in a special way in our home, and in our parish, and throughout the world. We pray to the Lord. All: Lord, hear our prayer.

Mother:

That our family may keep alive the spirit of our enthronement by gathering daily to renew our consecration, we pray to the Lord. All: Lord, hear our prayer.

Children:

For all the members of our family, we pray to the Lord. All: Lord, hear our prayer.

Family:

That we may ever give thanks to God for choosing our family to receive the gift of His presence and love, we pray to the Lord that our Enthronement shrine may ever remind us that Christ is King of our family, we pray to the Lord.

That God may bless our family with vocations to the priesthood and religious life, we pray to the Lord.

That each member of this family may have a deep and living faith through frequent celebration of the Eucharist together, we pray to the Lord.

That Our Blessed Mother and St. Joseph intercede for us that our family life may be based on that of the Holy Family, we pray to the Lord.

That the Enthronement may be known, understood, and requested in our parish community, we pray to the Lord.

Celebrant:

Sacred Heart of Jesus, You have promised to bless in a special way those families who honor Your Divine Heart in their home. Please shower Your blessings on this family which has invited You to preside over it as its King and to abide with it as its Friend. In Your Eucharistic Sacrifice we are about to offer, through You, with You, and in You, please present all our petitions to Your loving Father. Amen.

The signed certificate is carried to the altar during the Offeratory Procession.

Offertory Prayer and Hymn

Communion Prayer and Hymn

At the end of the Mass all say:

"The Lord shall be enthroned as King forever; the Lord shall bless His people with Peace." (Ps. 28)

The priest signs the "Covenant."

Recessional Hymn

Heart of Jesus, King and Savior

(Melody - Tantum Ergo: do, re, me, do)

Heart of Jesus, King and Savior,
Hear our prayer - Thy Kingdom Come!
In our family, school and parish
Be our friend, Our King of Love.
Through your Eucharistic banquet
Make our heart unite as one.

God the Father, Our Creator.
Loved us so, He gave His Son.
See the crib, the Cross, the Altar,
Proofs of love for everyone.
Heart of Jesus, send your Spirit.
Love's repaid by love alone.

Heart of Jesus, King and Brother,
In our home set up Your Throne.
Share our every joy and sorrow,
You we love and you alone.
Help us truly love our neighbor.
Make love reign in heart and home!

by Fr. Francis Larkin, SS.CC.
Imprimatur: Archbishop Thomas McDonough
Liturgical Committee

Family "Do it Yourself" Enthronement Ritual

Our Family Enthrones the Sacred Heart of Jesus As Our King, Provider and Friend.

(All are seated while the Father - or in his absence, mother - explains what is about to take place.)

Father: "You know, I think this might well be one of the most important gatherings of our life. The reason I say this is because I'm convinced from what we have been told and what I've read about the Enthronement, it brings terrific blessings to families. And the good Lord knows we need them.

"Actually what we are doing today is to invite Jesus to come into our home and to give Him a free hand. And we don't have to worry about what He does because He is the only one Who knows what He is doing and whatever He does is for our good, for He is the only one Who loves us and is our loyal and powerful friend.

"By the Enthronement, we are told, we enthrone Jesus as our King who rules over us through love — more like a Father than a ruler. He takes charge of all our affairs, big and small. He becomes our generous provider, Our Family Friend, Our spiritual physician, our financial advisor, our life insurer, our heavenly Banker, our constant Companion, the unseen Guest at every meal.

"And we want Him to be all these things because each and everyone of us need His help. It isn't easy to be good. We can't do it alone, but with Jesus' help we can make it.

"Isn't it wonderful to think that Jesus will be a real member of our family from now on? He comes into our home, not because we are better than anyone else, but because He knows how much we need Him. But if we expect Jesus to bless us, we have to promise to try harder to be good — to God, to each other and to those we meet outside of our home.

We hope that by what we are going to do today, and by the way we think of Jesus and talk with Him and trust Him in the future, that we will make up for so many families and so many people who don't love Jesus and are offending Him."

The Enthronement Ceremony

1. Father: Now let us all stand while in your name I enthrone the Sacred Heart as the Head of our Family.
   All gather around the father, who takes the Sacred Heart image and slowly walks over to the place prepared for it and enthrones it, that is, puts it on the "Throne")

   All: Jesus, You are the King and Friend of our family. We accept Your loving rule over us. Stay with us as our Friend. We need You.

   Father: Now we are going to say the Apostles Creed to make up for a lot of people we know who do not believe or practice what Jesus taught.

2. The Apostles Creed

   Father: Today we are going to turn our family over to the Sacred Heart of Jesus. When we were baptized we were dedicated to God. That is what we are going to do now - renew our dedication to God by consecrating ourselves to His loving Heart.

3. Act of Consecration

   Almighty and Eternal Father,/ we the (Smith) family,/ (then each member of the family says his first name beginning with the father) consecrates ourselves and our home to the Sacred Heart of Your Only Begoten Son/ who loves us with a tender and everlasting love./ May we return this love as He comes into the midst of our family/ to live and share our life in a special way from this day on.

   We accept you, Divine Heart of Jesus/ as a living member of this family./ Stay with us, Lord,/ Sanctify our joys and comfort us in all our sorrows./ May Your Holy Spirit inspire each of us so/ that we may be continually aware of Your special presence among us,/especially in one another./ Help us through this consecration/ to have a deep and loving respect for one another,/ So that we may daily live this consecration in our family life.

   Let our love go beyond our home into the world/ so that we may do our part/ to win other families to your Sacred Heart,/ thus helping to form a real community/

among the families of this parish/ and of the whole
world,

All: Sacred Heart of Jesus, we love you. Sacred Heart of
Jesus, Thy Kingdom come! Immaculate Heart of
Mary, Pray for us. Glory to the Sacred Heart of
Jesus forever and ever! Amen.

4. Short prayer of Intercession

Father: That the Sacred Heart of Jesus may be known
and loved and served in a special way, in our home,
in our neighborhood and in our parish, we pray to
the Lord, Lord, hear our prayer!

Mother: That Mary, Our Mother through her Immaculate Heart, help us keep the spirit of Our Enthronement by bringing us together daily to pray
in the name of Jesus, let us pray to the Lord; Lord,
hear our prayer!

Children: (or parents) : For all the members of our family who are not with us today, both living and
dead, let us pray to the Lord; Lord, hear our
prayer!

All: That God may bless our family with vocations to the
priesthood and religious life, Let us pray to the
Lord; Lord, hear our prayer!
(Note: Personal requests may be added, if desired.)

5. Litany of Thanksgiving

Father: Just as we thank God our heavenly Father,
through Jesus, His Son, during the Mass, so also
now we thank the Sacred Heart of Jesus through
the Heart of His mother.
We thank you, Lord.

Mother: For giving us our children.
We thank you, Lord.

Children: For giving us our parents,
We thank you, Lord.

Father: For coming to our hame,
We thank you, Lord.

Mother: For giving us Mary your mother, as our mother,
We thank you, Lord.

Children: For Our Holy Father, the Pope, Our Bishop,
our priests, our sisters and teachers,

We thank you, Lord.

Father: Now if there is anything special we would like
to thank Jesus for, now is the time to say it.

6. Hail Holy Queen

Father: Jesus is our King, Mary, His Mother is our
Queen. Many Catholics, by their deeds, their bad
talk, their immodesty, offend the Immaculate
Heart of our Queen. Let us make up for this and
at the same time promise our Mother that we will
try not to offend her.

Hail, Holy Queen, our life, our sweetness and our hope,
To you do we cry, poor banished children of Eve; to you
do we send up our cries, mourning and weeping in this
valley of tears. Turn then, most gracious advocate, your
eyes of mercy toward us, and after this exile, show us
the fruit of your womb, Jesus. O Clement, O Loving, O
sweet Virgin Mary! pray for us, O holy Mother of God,
that we may be made worthy of the promises of Christ.

7. All sign the Enthronement "Covenant" (certificate),
first, the father, then mother and then the children. It
is to be framed and hung near the Enthronement shrine.

8. Final Hymn

"Heart of Jesus, King and Savior"

(Melody: Tantum Ergo - do re mi do)

Heart of Jesus, King and Savior,
Hear our prayer - Thy Kingdom Come!
In our family, school and parish
Be our friend, Our King of Love.
Through your Eucharistic banquet
Make our heart unite as one.

God the Father, Our Creator.
Loved us so, He gave His Son.
See the crib, the Cross, the Altar,
Proofs of love for everyone.
Heart of Jesus, send your Spirit.
Love's repaid by love alone.

Heart of Jesus, King and Brother,
In our home set up Your Throne.
Share our every joy and sorrow,
You we love and you alone.
Help us truly love our neighbor.
Make love reign in heart and home!

9. The parents now give their children the parental blessing. The children kneel before the parents. First the father, then the mother, make a sign of the Cross on the forehead of each child, saying: "I bless you, my child, in the name of the Father, and of the Son, and of the Holy Spirit." The child answers, "Amen."

10. In honor of the divine guest, refreshments will now be served.

DAILY PRAYERS

The Mystical Mass Prayer - By Luke Zimmer, SS.CC.

Saint Michael, the Archangel, defend us in battle, be our safeguard against the wickedness and snares of the devil. May God rebuke him we humbly pray; and do you, Prince of the heavenly host, by the power of God, cast into hell Satan and all the evil spirits, who wander through the world seeking the ruin of souls.

Most Sacred Heart of Jesus, have mercy on us (three times).

I wish to invite each angel and saint in heaven and the souls in purgatory to pray with me and for me.

Eternal Father, I offer to you through the Immaculate and Sorrowful Heart of Mary, in the Holy Spirit, the Body, Blood, Soul and Divinity of your Divine Son, Jesus Christ, from all the altars throughout the world at each Holy Mass which is celebrated on this day and every day until the end of time.

To each Mass, I wish to unite everything that took place in the lives of Jesus, Mary, and Joseph while they lived on earth (think of the things in detail or in general) and their existence in heaven for all eternity.

I wish to unite everything which took place in the life of each angel in heaven(creation, trial, victory, glory, and joy in heaven, the honor and glory given to God.)

I wish to unite everything good in the life of each person in purgatory, and the happiness they will enjoy in heaven, and the honor and glory they will give to you.

I wish to unite every good thought, word, and deed in the life of each person who is living and will live until the end of time.

I wish to unite the honor and glory of all creation.

Finally, I wish to unite myself with Christ in each Mass which I offer to you. Take me and do with me what you wish, when you wish, and as long as you wish. Give me the serenity to accept the things I cannot change, the courage to change the things I can, and the wisdom to know the difference.

Help me to love you, My God, with all my heart and soul, with all my strength and mind and my neighbor as myself for the love of you.

I wish to accept the type of death you wish me to die, when, where, how and why.

I offer all through Him, with Him, in Him, in the unity of the Holy Spirit for your glory and honor, Almighty Father, forever and ever.

Let each Mass be an act of love and adoration which I wish to offer to you, God the Father, since you are Our God, Our Creator, and Our Father — My Father. To you, God the Son, since you are our God, Our Redeemer, Mediator, King, Judge, and Brother — My Brother. To you, God the Holy Spirit, since You are our God, our Advocate, our Paraclete, our Sanctifier — my Holy Spirit.

Let each Holy Mass be an act of thanksgiving for all the gifts and graces given to each person and each one who will exist, especially for . . . . .

Let each Holy Mass be an act of reparation for all the sins that have, are, and will be committed, until the end of the world. Especially sins of ingratitude, indifference, unbelief, swearing, cursing, blasphemy, sacrilege, anger, hatred, murder, and all sins of impurity; especially for my sins of. . . . .

From each Holy Mass, O Triune God, I ask you to bless my father, mother, sisters, brothers, relatives, friends, and especially. . . . .

Bless the Holy Father, the Pope; the cardinals, bishops, priests, sisters, brothers and all those aspiring to serve you in religious life, especially. . . . . .and may more and more aspire to God's service.

Bless the poor, the sick, the dying, and the poor souls in Purgatory.

Bless and cure. . . . . .

Let each Holy Mass be a petition for peace, and for an increase of faith, hope, and love.

Cum Permissu:
>   Harold Meyer, SS.CC.
>   Provincial of Hawaii

Nihil Obstat:
>   John B. Reed
>   Censor Librorum

Imprimatur:
>   John J. Scanlan, D.D.
>   Bishop of Honolulu

December 8, 1968

Chaplet of the Holy Spirit

Homage Of Adoration to the Paraclete

in Honor of His Seven Gifts

Since this is the age of the Holy Spirit, here is a practical suggestion for a simple, yet beautiful, way of honoring the Holy Spirit and drawing His sevenfold gifts upon us.

Let us endeavor to instill, in the first place, love of the Paraclete, as a strong and doctrinal devotion suitable to the choicest among pious souls.

Let us, therefore, form the praiseworthy habit of reciting the Chaplet which is proposed here, as an homage to the Holy Spirit.

Come, Holy Spirit, enlighten my mind! Come, inflame my heart!

1. Take your beads (the Blessed Virgin's rosary) and recite the Apostles' Creed.

2. After the Creed, very slowly and devoutly, the Glory be to the Father.

3. Then say the Our Father.

4. Now, very fervently, say this ejaculation: "Father, send us the promised Paraclete, through Jesus Christ our Lord. Amen."

5. Now on each bead, instead of the Hail Mary say with a burning heart: "Come, Holy Spirit, fill the hearts of your faithful and kindle in them the fire of your love!"

6. After the tenth bead recite the following official prayer: "Send forth your Spirit and they shall be created, and you shall renew the face of the earth.

O God, who did instruct the hearts of the faithful by the light of the Holy Spirit, grant us by the same Spirit to be truly wise and evermore to rejoice in His consolations. Through Christ our Lord. Amen.

7. Then recite the second decade and all the others in the same way as explained (beginning at 3) : "Our Father"

8. After the seventh and last decade, recite the "Hail, Holy Queen" in honor of the Blessed Virgin, our Heavenly Queen, who presided in the Cenacle on the Great Sunday of Pentecost.

A few short reflections may be made on seven glorious mysteries relating to seven wonderful operations of the Paraclete. These meditations should be made briefly, between every ten beads.

1st Mystery: Let us honor the Holy Spirit and adore Him who is love substantial, proceeding from the Father and the Son, and uniting Them in an infinite and eternal charity.

2nd Mystery: Let us honor the operation of the Holy Spirit and adore Him in the Immaculate Conception of Mary, sanctifying her, from the first moment with the plentitude of grace.

3rd Mystery: Let us honor the operation of the Holy Spirit and adore Him in the Incarnation of the Word, the Son of God by his Divine Nature, and the Son of the Virgin by the flesh.

4th Mystery: Let us honor the operation of the Holy Spirit and adore Him giving birth to the Church on the glorious day of Pentecost in the Cenacle.

5th Mystery: Let us honor the operation of the Holy Spirit and adore Him dwelling in the Church and assisting her faithfully according to the Divine promise, even to the consummation of the world.

6th Mystery: Let us honor the wonderful operation of the Holy Spirit creating within the Church that other Christ, the priest, and conferring the plentitude of the priesthood on the Bishops.

7th Mystery: Let us honor the operation of the Holy Spirit and adore Him in the heroic virtue of the saints in the Church, that hidden and marvelous work of the "Adorable Sanctifier."

Practices:

Recite the Chaplet of the Holy Spirit often, even daily.

Recite it:

1. Especially on Sundays

2. When some important decision must be made; at certain grave moments and when special spiritual help is needed.

3. As a preparation for the Feast of Pentecost; this day witnessed birth of the Church of Christ.

4. Every day during recollections and retreats.

Written by Father Mateo, SS.CC.

Imprimatur:

Carolus Hubertus Le Blond
Bishop of St. Joseph

The Rosary

Monday and Thursdays: *Joyful Mysteries*

1. Annunciation
2. Visitation
3. Nativity
4. Presentation
5. Finding of Jesus in the Temple

Tuesday and Friday: *Sorrowful Mysteries*

1. Agony in the Garden
2. Scourging
3. Crowning with Thorns
4. Carrying the Cross
5. Crucifixion

Sunday, Wednesday,
   and Saturday: *Glorious Mysteries*

1. Resurrection
2. Ascension
3. Descent of the Holy Spirit
4. Assumption of the Blessed Virgin Mary
5. Crowning of the Blessed Virgin Mary in heaven.

Renewal of Total Committment to Jesus through Mary

In the presence of all the heavenly court, 1, n. . . . . choose you today as my Mother. I deliver and consecrate myself to you completely; my body and soul, my goods, both interior an dexterior, and even the value of all my good actions, past, present, and future.

I also renew and ratify today in your hands, O Immaculate Mother, the vows of my baptism; I renounce forever Satan, his pomps and works.

Through your hands, O Blessed Mother, I consecrate and commit myself entirely to Jesus Christ, your Son and my Brother, to carry my cross after Him all the days of my life, and to be more faithful to Him than ever before.

Grant that I may be faithful in living this commitment every day of my life. Amen.

Renewal Prayer of the Consecration of the Family to the Immaculate Heart

Queen of the most holy Rosary, and tender Mother of men,/ to fulfill the desires of the Sacred Heart,/ and the request of the Vicar of your Son on earth,/ we renew our consecration to you, and to your Immaculate Heart,/ and recommend to you,/ all the families of our nation and of all the world.

Please accept our consecration, dearest Mother,/ and use us and all families as you wish,/ to accomplish your designs upon the world.

O Immaculate Heart of Mary,/ Queen of heaven and earth, and our family,/ rule over us, together with the Sacred Heart of Jesus Christ, our King./ Save us from the spreading flood of modern paganism, kindle in our hearts and homes the love of purity,/ and practice of the Christian life,/ and an ardent zeal for souls, and for the holiness of family life.

We come with confidence to you,/ O Throne of Grace and Mother of Fair Love;/ inflame us with the same divine fire/ which has inflamed your own Immaculate Heart.

Make our hearts and homes your shrine,/ and through us make the Heart of Jesus/ rule and triumph in every family in the world. Amen.

Renewal Prayer of the Enthronement of the
Sacred Heart of Jesus

Most sweet Jesus, humbly kneeling at thy feet,/ we renew the consecration of our family to the Divine Heart.

Be thou our King forever,/ In Thee we have full and entire confidence./ May thy Spirit penetrate our thoughts,/ our desires,/ our words and our deeds./ Bless our undertakings,/ share in our joys, in our trials,/ in our labors.

Grant us to know Thee better,/ to love thee more,/ to serve Thee without faltering.

By the Immaculate Heart of Mary, Queen of Peace,/ set up Thy Kingdom in our country./ Enter closely into the midst of our families and make them thine own/ through the solemn Enthronement of thy Sacred Heart,/ so that soon one cry may resound from home to home./ May the Triumphant Heart of Jesus be everywhere loved,/ blessed, and glorified forever./ To the Sacred Hearts of Jesus and Mary/ be honor and glory forever and ever.

Sacred Heart of Jesus, protect our families.

Catalogue of Religious Books, Booklets, Articles

1. E.rec   LP Record on Enthronement ....$ 4.00

2. E-Film "The Sacred Heart Enthroned"
   Enthronement Film............................Rental   10.00
                                    Purchase 100.00

3. SH Bad   Badge of the Sacred Hearts................   .10

4. Companion Pictures (Laminated) 9.00
   SH-3   Sacred Heart 13-1/2 x 16-1/2
   IHM-3 Immaculate Heart 13-1/2 x 16-1/2

5. SH-2   Sacred Heart, Jesus King of Love 1.50
   10-1/2 x 13-1/2

6. IMH-2   Immaculate Heart 10-1/2 x 13-1/2 .... 1.50

7. Fire "The Firebrand"
   By Father Francis Larkin, SS.CC. 4.00

8. Little Chaplet of the Holy Spirit .... .05

9. Family Prayer Renewal in the Heart of Christ
                              Blue Booklet............   .20
                              Green Booklet 25

10. Official MSH lapel pin 1.00

11. Jesus, King of Love, by Fr. Mateo, SS.CC. 2.00

12. Enthronement of the Sacred Heart, Fr. Larkin,
                                    SS.CC. 2.00

13. Kit - Fd - 4 Copies of Cerem. 1.50
    Sh - 5

14. Na - Night Adoration
    MHWJ - My Hour with Jesus
    HH-R - Holy Hour - Religious
    HH-RC - Holy Hour - Religious Communities
    NA-RN - Holy Hour Nurses
    NA-Col - Holy Hour College Students
    FHH - Family Holy Hour ....Each   .25

National Center of the Enthronement
3 Adams St.
Fairhaven, Mass. 02719

The Imitation of Christ, by Thomas A. Kempis .... .85
  Image Books
  A Division of Doubleday & Company, Inc.
  Garden City, N.Y.

7-Color Lithograph of the Sacred Heart .... .05
  Size 7-1/2 x 12-1/2
  Order in lots of 50 or 100
  Messenger Corporation
  Auburn, Indiana 46706

Color Portraits of the Sacred Heart 3/ 1.00
  Size 8 x 10   10/ 2.00
  The Woeber Family
  Box 45441(A)
  Dallas, Texas 75235

Prayer for a Holy Hour .... .10
  Benedictine Convent of Perpetual Adoration
  Clyde, Missouri 64432

Outlines of the 16 Documents of Vatican II .... .65
  The Long Island Catholic
  53 North Park Avenue
  Rockville Center, N.Y. 11570

The Sacred Heart Renewal in the Heart of Christ .... .50
                              (10 or more)   .40
                              (100 or more) .30

  Marytown Press
  8000 39th Ave.
  Kenosha, Wis. 52141

The Documents of Vatican II .... .95
  By Walter M. Abbott, S.J.
  Boromeo Guild
  1530 W. 9th St.
  Los Angeles, Calif. 90015

The Apostolate of Christian Renewal 1.00
  Apostolate of Christian Renewal
  14341 Fairgrove Ave.
  La Puente, Calif. 91746